by

Liza Huber

Sage Spoonfuls™

Simple Recipes * Healthy Meals * Happy Babies

Photography by Basia Ambroziak

Sage Bears Books

SIMPLE

RECIPES

*

HEALTHY

MEALS

*

HAPPY

BABIES

ROYCE, 6 BRENDAN, 4 HAYDEN, 2 MASON, 1

Welcome To Sage Spoonfuls!

As parents, we only want the best for our children. By feeding them homemade baby food, we are not only giving them the most delicious and nutritious food—we are laying a strong foundation for a lifetime of healthy choices.

You don't need to be a chef, have a lot of time on your hands, or a kitchen full of fancy equipment to make your own baby food—in fact you'll be shocked at how fun and easy it is with the Sage Spoonfuls system. By spending just 1 hour every 2 weeks, you can have a freezer stocked with healthy and delicious baby food. Instead of going to the store to buy baby food, you can simply "go shopping" in your freezer!

You won't find time-consuming or fancy recipes in this book. What you will find are easy-to-prepare whole foods that are delicious on their own or mixed together to make endless yummy combinations. By keeping it simple, you keep it easy. There are even a number of purees that can be whipped up in seconds!

The idea for Sage Spoonfuls was born when I had my first baby. I searched high and low and could not find homemade baby food products that offered the ease of use, convenience, and quality I was looking for. I created Sage Spoonfuls so parents would have a complete homemade baby food system. One that had the same convenience as store-bought, but with the enormous benefits of homemade. I hope you enjoy Sage Spoonfuls as much as I enjoyed creating it!

Liza

THE MENU

FOOD FOR THOUGHT

CHAPTER ONE

Why Make Your Own Baby Food?

Homemade baby food is the most nutritious

Store bought baby food, including the organic brands, has a shelf life of between 18 months and 2 years! In order to achieve this shelf life, the food needs to be sterilized. This is accomplished by heating it to very high temperatures to ensure food safety. While sterilization is necessary to achieve shelf life, it kills vitamins, nutrients, taste, color, and aroma in the process. Homemade baby food is higher in nutrients, tastes far better than store bought, and has the enticing aroma that will make your baby excited about eating. Homemade baby food can retain most of its nutritional value, taste, color, texture, and aroma because it is only lightly steamed and not overcooked. In fact, most ripe fruits can be pureed without cooking, leaving all of the precious nutrients intact!

Commercially prepared baby food often contains additives and fillers that have no nutritional value. These additives and fillers have the potential to cause allergic reactions in children and can also contribute to hyperactivity. Not to mention, why would we want to feed our infants additives and empty calories? There are no additives, fillers, or empty calories in homemade baby food. By making your own you have control over the ingredients. You know where the food came from, because you bought it and you know exactly what is in the food, because you made it.

With childhood obesity at an all time high, it is more important than ever to give our children the most nutritious food right from the start. The healthy eating habits we introduce to our babies now will benefit them for the rest of their lives.

Homemade baby food is the most economical

Buying commercially prepared baby food can get very expensive, especially if you have more than 1 child. Depending on the brand, store bought baby food can cost two to three times more than homemade! Not to mention the dollars wasted when you throw away a jar or pouch of half eaten food.

The best way to save money on baby food is to make it yourself in large batches and store it in Sage Spoonfuls jars in the refrigerator or freezer. You save money while giving your child the most nutritious and best tasting food.

What could be better than that? My favorite example is with butternut squash: 1 large butternut squash costs about $3.50 but yields 25 ounces of baby food!

Homemade baby food leads to more adventurous eaters!

Babies do not need to eat bland food. They are far more adventurous eaters if given the opportunity. Commercially prepared baby food is usually bland in color, taste, and texture. Additionally, the smell of store bought baby food is rarely as enticing as homemade. Babies who are fed a consistent diet of this food have a much higher chance of becoming picky eaters in the future. They become so accustomed to eating bland food, which they don't enjoy very much, that they are less eager to try new tastes and textures. Unfortunately, this pattern often continues into the toddler years and well into childhood. How many young children do you know who won't eat anything other than processed chicken nuggets?

On the other hand, babies who are fed a consistent diet of delicious homemade baby food often grow to become adventurous eaters who make healthy choices for themselves without even realizing it. When my boys want a snack, they usually reach for an apple. They are too young to know that apples are healthy; they just know they love the taste. This is not to say kids who are fed homemade baby food won't go crazy for ice cream, cookies and chicken nuggets on occasion; it's just that getting them to eat well isn't a daily struggle.

Your baby's taste buds and palate are developing during the first year of life. The more tastes, textures and yummy smells you can expose your baby to, the better. With store bought baby food, we are only given a handful of choices for each stage—usually whatever the manufacturer thinks is the most popular. With homemade baby food the yummy flavor combinations are almost endless. Your baby will enjoy mealtime instead of seeing it as a chore.

Try doing a taste test at home. Once you taste and smell a freshly mashed banana vs. a processed baby food banana—you'll be hooked on homemade.

Why Make Your Own Baby Food?

Homemade baby food is the "green" choice

With commercially prepared baby food, there is the constant purchasing and discarding of jars, lids, pouches, or boxes. Can you imagine how many baby food containers get thrown away in a year? Plus, the epoxy lining in the metal caps of baby food jars often contains BPA, a known hormone disruptor. Not to mention the wasted food that gets thrown out from an unfinished meal.

By making your own baby food and storing it in Sage Spoonfuls jars, you are not adding waste to the environment, exposing your child to Bisphenol-A, or wasting food.

If you are making your baby food with organic produce, you are doing further good for the environment (and your baby) by supporting farmers who do not grow their fruits and vegetables with the use of environmentally harmful chemicals and pesticides.

Additionally, it takes far less energy to make your own baby food than a large factory making baby food, that needs to then be transported all over the country.

Homemade baby food is just as convenient as store bought

The Sage Spoonfuls system makes homemade baby food just as convenient as store-bought. By preparing your baby's food in large batches and storing it in the refrigerator or freezer, you will have a constant available stock of healthy and delicious food.

Sage Spoonfuls jars, trays and labels make storing homemade baby food an easy one-step process. There are no messy ice cube trays or pop open lids to deal with. Sage Spoonfuls jars are also the perfect size. Most jars you'll find have a small 2 ounce capacity; Sage Spoonfuls jars have a convenient 4 ounce capacity and are also ideal for serving your baby food when away from home.

Taking homemade baby food on-the-go is easy with Sage Spoonfuls. The insulated bags and reusable freezer packs keep food fresh for up to 12 hours so your baby can have delicious and healthy homemade baby food no matter where the day takes him!

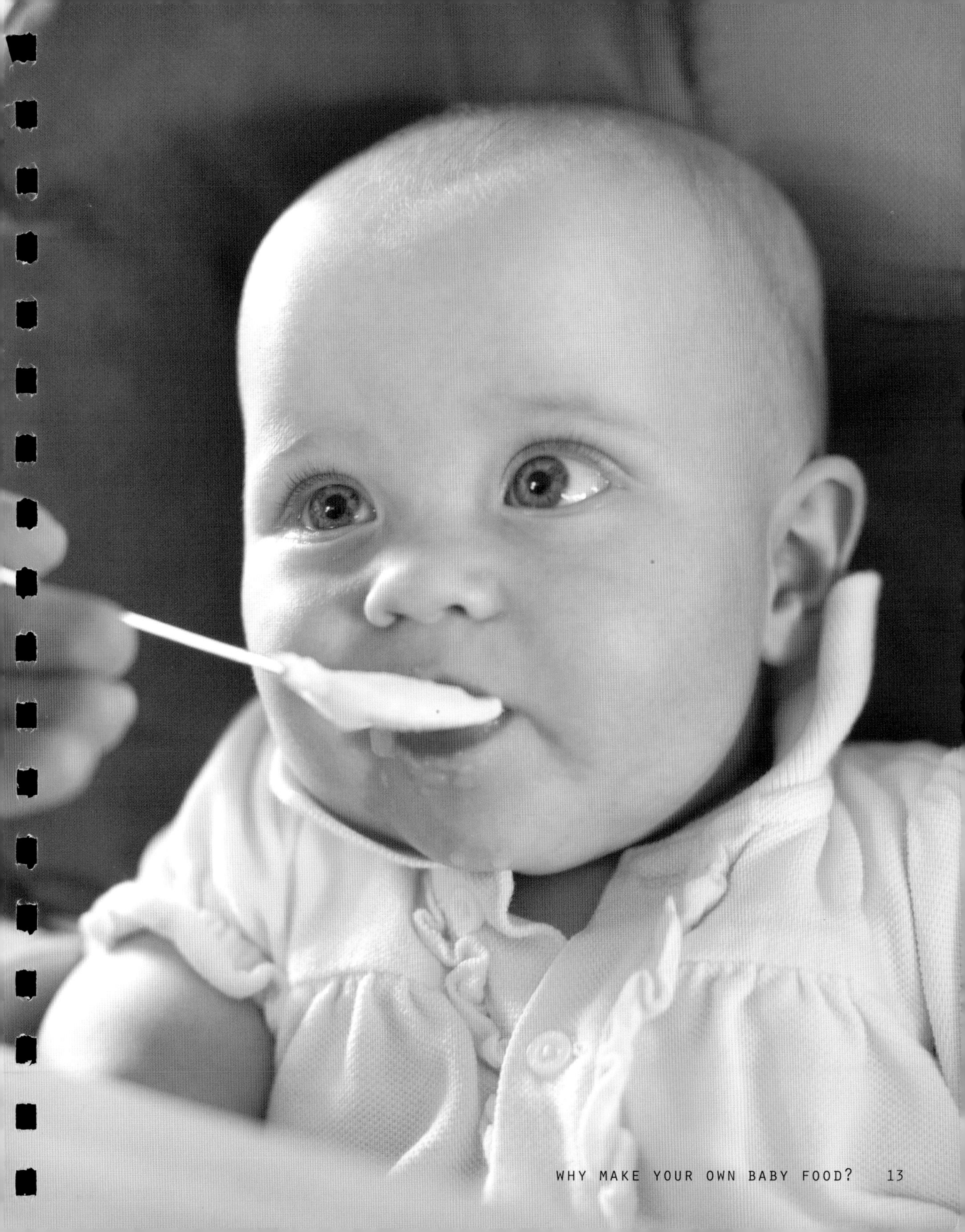

The Benefits of Going Organic

Organic fruits and vegetables are grown without the use of harmful pesticides and fertilizers and are not genetically engineered or modified in any way. Many chemical pesticides are known to contain carcinogens, suspected hormone disruptors, and neurotoxins. Scientists now believe that even small doses of these harmful pesticides can have lasting negative effects on your child's health.

In 2005, the USDA Pesticide Data Program found 42 different pesticide residues on conventionally grown apple samples. These standard chemicals can be up to 10 times more toxic to children than adults, because children ingest more toxins relative to body weight. They also have vulnerable developing organ systems that are less able to detoxify these chemicals. In addition to being a safer choice for our children, some recent studies have found organic fruits and vegetables to be higher in nutrients than conventionally grown. Many people say that organic produce even tastes better.

Organic fruits and vegetables are readily available in most food stores. While they still cost more than conventionally grown, the prices are dropping rapidly due to consumer demand. As far as selection goes, your best bet would be an organic or natural grocery store. However, these stores can be fairly pricey. Large grocery chains have recognized the growing movement toward organics and carry a wider selection than you might think. They also tend to have more competitive prices than smaller, specialty markets. Farmers markets are also a great choice, because they are less expensive than specialty stores, plus you get the added benefit of supporting your local farmers. Visit www.localharvest.org for organic farmers markets near you.

When shopping for organic fruits and veggies, look for a 5 digit number beginning with 9 on the sticker or package. Also look for a "USDA ORGANIC" mark on the package. Beware of any product claiming to be "natural," "wholesome" or "made with natural ingredients", if it does not have USDA certification. There are many imposter items on the market and only those with a USDA mark are truly organic.

The Benefits of Going Organic

If buying organic is not an option, you can still greatly reduce the amount of pesticide residue on your fruits and veggies by washing them thoroughly under cold running water and peeling. Additionally, whenever possible, buy produce that was grown in the USA. We have stricter guidelines regarding pesticide use than many other countries.

Whether you use organic or conventionally grown fruits and veggies, you are giving your child the gift of the most delicious and nutritious food there is—homemade.

The Benefits of Going Organic

The Dirty Dozen and Clean 15

The *Environmental Working Group*, a non-profit environmental research organization, releases a yearly guide that lists which conventionally grown fruits and vegetables have the most pesticide residue and which have the least. You can cut your family's pesticide exposure dramatically if you buy the foods on the "dirty dozen" list organic.

12 Most Contaminated – a.k.a. "Dirty Dozen"
(buy these organic as often as possible)

1. Apples
2. Celery
3. Strawberries
4. Peaches
5. Spinach
6. Nectarines (imported)
7. Grapes (imported)
8. Bell peppers
9. Potatoes
10. Blueberries (domestic)
11. Lettuce
12. Kale

15 Least Contaminated – a.k.a. "Clean Fifteen"
(lowest in pesticides)

1. Onions
2. Sweet Corn
3. Pineapple
4. Avocado
5. Asparagus
6. Sweet Peas
7. Mangoes
8. Eggplant
9. Canteloupe (domestic)
10. Kiwi
11. Cabbage
12. Watermelon
13. Sweet Potatoes
14. Grapefruit
15. Mushrooms

These lists are updated each year; please visit www.ewg.org for future reference.

For more information on pesticides visit:
www.organicconsumers.com – Organic Consumers Association
www.whatsonmyfood.org
www.epa.gov – Environmental Protection Agency
www.panna.org – Pesticide Action Network of North America

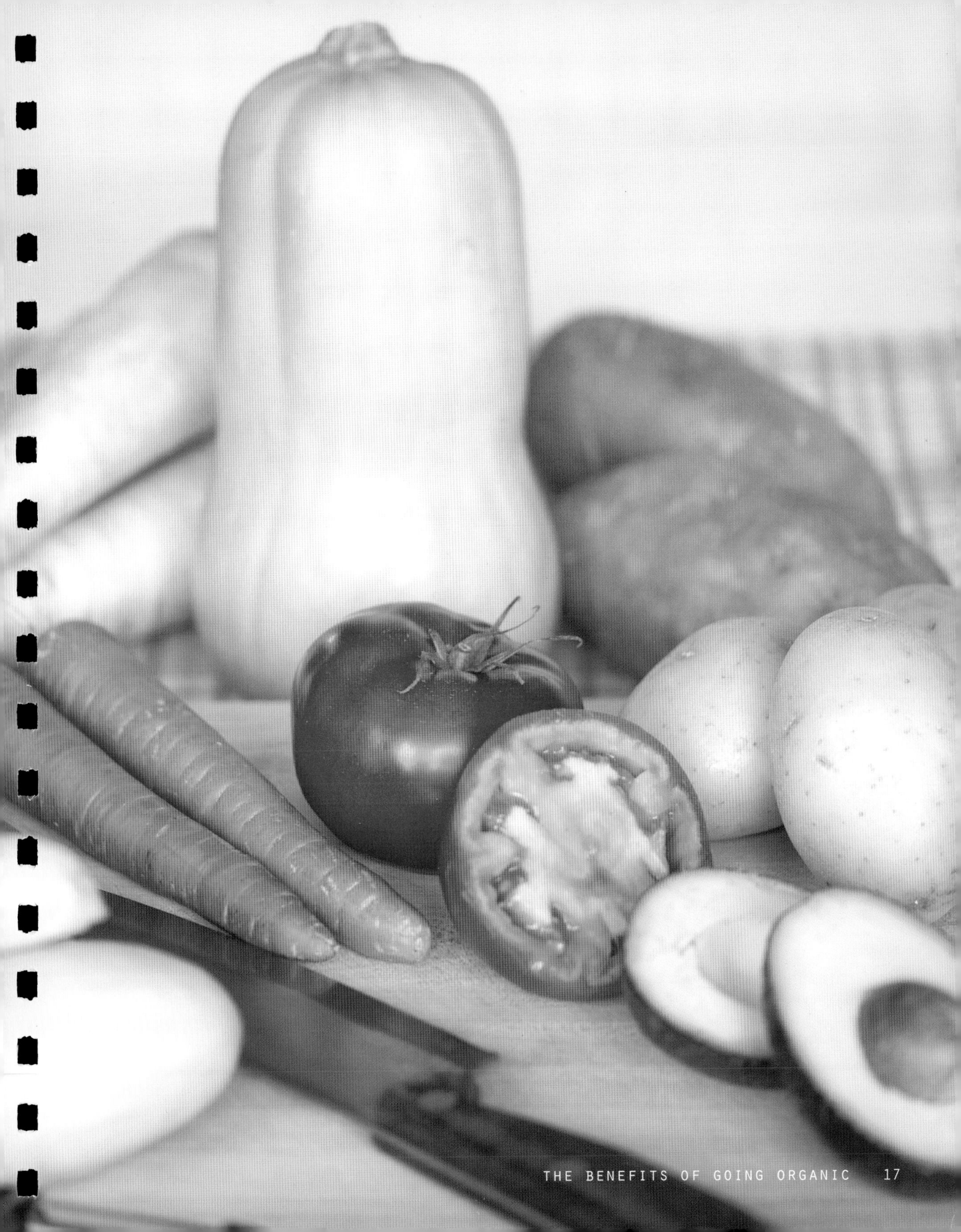

THE
ESSENTIALS

Allergies and Food Intolerances

Before starting your baby on solids, discuss any family history of allergies or food intolerances with your child's pediatrician. It is important to note that your baby can have an allergic reaction to a food, even if there is no family history. Introduce foods one at a time, for about 3 days each, so if your baby has an adverse reaction, you will know what caused it. Before combining foods, make sure your baby has tried each one, individually.

If you suspect your baby is having an adverse reaction to a certain food, discontinue the food immediately and call your child's pediatrician.

Food Intolerance

Food intolerance is a digestive system issue. It happens when the digestive system can't break down the food properly because of a reaction to a naturally occurring chemical in the food, a lack of the proper digestive enzymes, or if your baby's body has an adverse reaction to a certain food additive. Food intolerances are not life threatening, but they should be brought to your pediatrician's attention for further guidance. You will most likely be able to reintroduce the food when your baby is older. Signs your baby could be suffering from food intolerance:

* Irritability
* Nausea
* Vomiting
* Diarrhea
* Gas
* Cramps
* Bloating

Food Allergy

Food allergies are an immune system issue. When the immune system reacts negatively to a certain food protein, it produces antibodies called immunoglobulins and an allergic reaction occurs. Roughly 6% of children in the United States have diagnosed food allergies.

If your child does have a food allergy, it is very important to advise caregivers, friends, family, daycare, and anyone who will be caring for your child. Be sure they are aware of the allergy and how to handle a reaction should one occur. If your child would require an EpiPen or Twinject, make sure the caregiver knows how to use it.

An allergic reaction may occur within a few minutes or may take a few hours. Food allergies can range from mild to very serious—even life threatening. Signs of a possible food allergy include:

* Pale Skin
* Loss of Energy
* Rash, Hives, or Itchy Skin
* Nausea, Vomiting, or Diarrhea
* Sneezing
* Coughing or Wheezing
* Difficulty Breathing
* Anaphylaxis

* If you notice that your baby is having difficulty breathing, hoarseness, swelling of the tongue or mouth or has a sudden loss of energy call 911 immediately because it could be anaphylaxis. Anaphylaxis is a life threatening reaction to a food that requires immediate medical attention including the administering of an EpiPen or Twinject.

Most Allergic Foods

The old school of thought was that parents should wait until their baby is at least 12 months old to introduce foods considered to be highly allergenic. There is currently much debate as to whether this is accurate or not. According to the American Academy of Pediatrics, there is no current convincing evidence that delaying the introduction of foods considered to be highly allergenic has any protective effect on the development of a food allergy. In fact, in the 2009 *American Academy of Pediatrics Journal*, it was reported that "the early consumption of peanuts in infancy is associated with a low prevalence of peanut allergies." For example, in a study published in the October 2008 *The Journal of Allergy and Clinical Immunology*, it was found that children living in Israel, introduced to peanut protein between 8–14 months of age, had a much lower incidence of peanut allergies than children belonging to the same ethnic group, in the United Kingdom, who were not introduced to peanut protein until they were 2 or sometimes 3 years old.

The subject of children's food allergies is one of great importance. Currently, there are no conclusive answers as to why the percentage of American children with food allergies is on the rise. I recommend discussing the introduction of these foods with your pediatrician to decide what is right for your baby.

Allergies and Food Intolerances

Most Allergenic Foods

The foods listed below account for 90% of food allergies:

* Cow's Milk
* Soy
* Egg Whites
* Peanuts
* Tree nuts (walnuts, pecans, cashews, etc)
* Fish
* Shellfish
* Wheat

The majority of children with cow's milk, soy, wheat, or egg allergies will eventually outgrow them. You will most likely be able to reintroduce these foods, with a pediatrician's guidance, when the time is right. However, some allergies, like peanut, tree nut, and shellfish may last a lifetime.

A wheat allergy is not the same as actual gluten intolerance. A child can outgrow a wheat allergy, whereas gluten intolerance lasts a lifetime and needs to be carefully managed.

For more information on food allergies and intolerances:
www.Foodallergy.org – Food Allergy and Anaphylaxis Network
www.AAP.org – American Academy of Pediatrics
www.AAAAI.org – American Academy of Allergy, Asthma, and Immunology
www.celiac.org – Celiac Disease Foundation

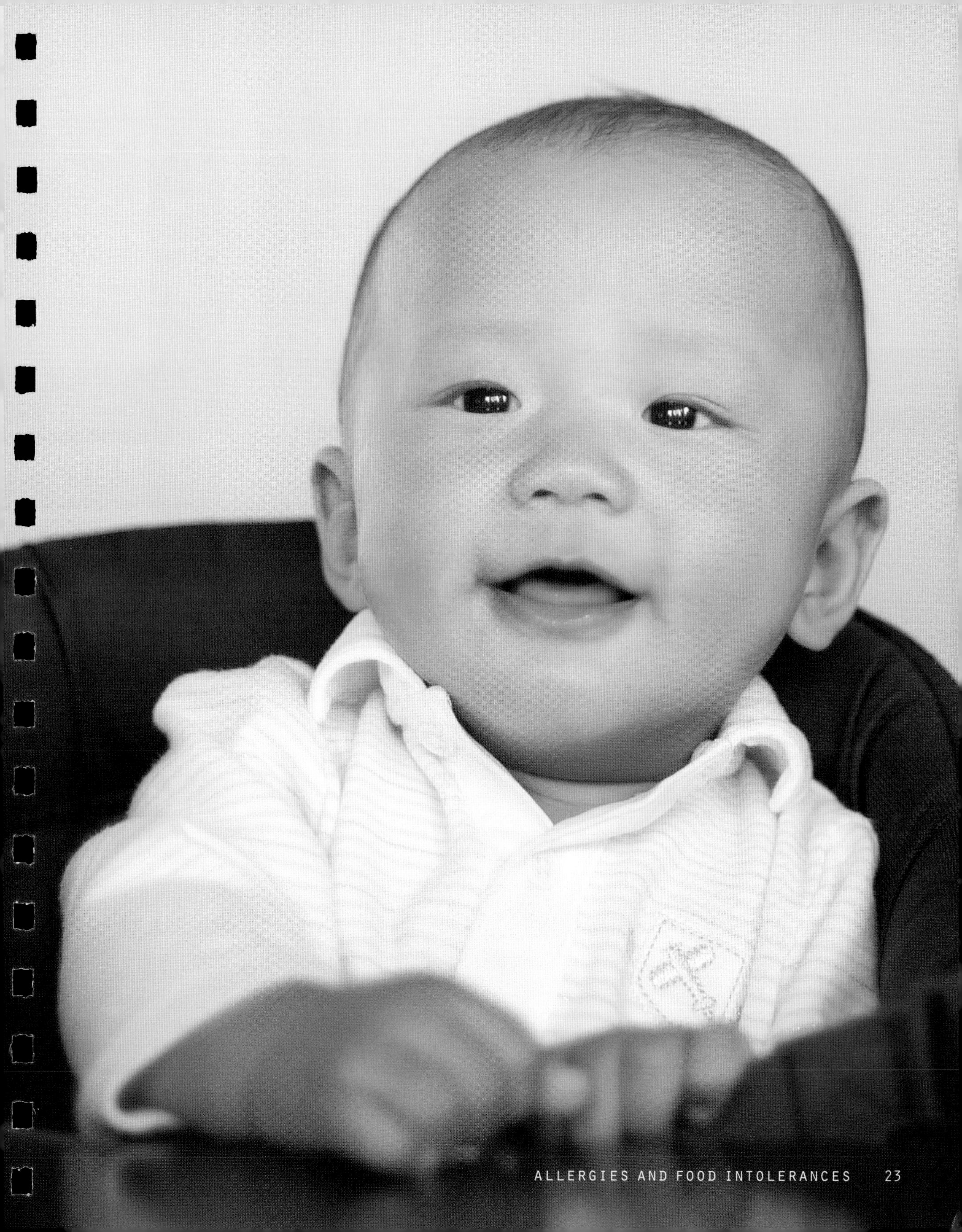

The ABC's of Good Nutrition

During your baby's first year of life, breast milk or formula will be her primary source of nutrition, but her diet should be supplemented with solid food, starting around 4–6 months. Not only is it beneficial to expose her to a variety of tastes and textures during this first year—it is essential to her growth and future health to have a strong nutritional foundation.

Vitamins
Vitamins are an important component to your baby's healthy growth and development. They are categorized as either fat-soluble or water-soluble. Fat-soluble vitamins are stored in the body and can be used as a reserve if not replenished daily, while water-soluble vitamins are not stored in the body and need to be replenished on a daily basis.

Fat-Soluble

Vitamin A – Essential for the immune system, helps fight off infection, and is important for nerve cell function and cell growth. It also helps promote healthy eyes, teeth, and skin. Vitamin A from plant foods is called Beta-Carotene and is an antioxidant that helps protect cells from damage. It can be found in sweet potatoes, spinach, broccoli, leeks, green beans, carrots, peas, tomatoes, sweet red peppers, butternut squash, pumpkin, dried apricots, mangoes, and cantaloupe.

Vitamin D – Essential for building strong bones by regulating how the body absorbs calcium. Babies need more vitamin D than adults because their bones are growing so quickly. Formula, yogurt, cheese, and other foods are often fortified with vitamin D; however, naturally occurring vitamin D can be found in sunlight, breast milk, fish, and egg yolks.

Vitamin E – A natural antioxidant that helps guard against cancer, heart disease, and other conditions by protecting cells from damage. It can be found in avocado, tomatoes, spinach, asparagus, pumpkin, butternut squash, sweet red peppers, parsnips, broccoli, prunes, kiwi, beef, and salmon.

Vitamin K – Essential in helping blood to clot. Most babies are given a vitamin K shot at birth to help prevent hemorrhage. Vitamin K is also important to bone health. It can be found in spinach, parsnips, lettuce, broccoli, peas, asparagus, celery, green beans, cauliflower, carrots, green beans, zucchini, leeks, potatoes, chickpeas, prunes, avocados, pears, raspberries, blueberries, grapes, oats, and beef.

Thiamin (Vitamin B1) – Essential for energy production, nerve cell function, and carbohydrate metabolism. It can be found in salmon, pork, lamb, beef, lentils, soybeans, chickpeas, black beans, lima beans, corn, asparagus, sweet potatoes, parsnips, butternut squash, peas, potatoes, carrots, avocados, bananas, pineapple, millet, oats, barley, quinoa, and brown rice.

Riboflavin (Vitamin B2) – Essential for energy production. It can be found in mushrooms, peas, asparagus, potatoes, zucchini, sweet potatoes, pumpkin, avocados, soybeans, lentils, chickpeas, black beans, lima beans, salmon, pork, lamb, beef, prunes, bananas, eggs, oats, and quinoa.

Niacin (Vitamin B3) – Essential for energy production and carbohydrate metabolism. It can be found in fish, pork, lamb, turkey, chicken, beef, soybeans, lentils, chickpeas, black beans, lima beans, parsnips, butternut squash, peas, carrots, potatoes, avocados, bananas, prunes, eggs, brown rice, millet, and barley.

Pantothenic Acid (Vitamin B5) – Essential for energy and red blood cell production. It can be found in corn, avocados, mushrooms, broccoli, cauliflower, sweet potatoes, parsnips, butternut squash, potatoes, lima beans, soybeans, lentils, chickpeas, black beans, salmon, pork, lamb, beef, bananas, oats, and brown rice.

Vitamin B6 – Helps the body make red blood cells and metabolize proteins and fats. Also aids in immune and nervous system function and proper hormonal balance. It can be found in bananas, avocados, pineapple, kiwi, cantaloupe, mangoes, prunes, potatoes, carrots, zucchini, sweet red pepper, broccoli, squash, tomatoes, leeks, butternut squash, peas, potatoes, cauliflower, sweet potatoes, lentils, chickpeas, lima beans, soybeans, fish, poultry, meat, quinoa, brown rice, amaranth, millet, and barley.

The ABC's of Good Nutrition

Vitamins   **Water-Soluble** (Continued)

Folic Acid (Folate) – Essential for all cell functions including the development of the nervous system. It is critically important that pregnant women get enough folic acid, because it helps to build a healthy spinal cord and lowers the risk of neural tube defects in the baby, such as spina bifida. Folic acid can be found in parsnips, butternut squash, peas, potatoes, zucchini, beets, green beans, cauliflower, mushrooms, leeks, broccoli, asparagus, sweet red pepper, spinach, corn, avocados, bananas, cantaloupe, strawberries, papaya, kiwi, blackberries, dates, salmon, beef, lima beans, soybeans, lentils, chickpeas, black beans, barley, millet, amaranth, quinoa, and oats.

Vitamin B12 – Works together with folic acid. It is essential for the formation of red blood cells and proper nerve function and development. It can be found in cottage cheese, fish, pork, lamb, turkey, chicken, beef, eggs, and cheese.

Vitamin C – One of the main functions of vitamin C is to make collagen, which is the essential protein substance in our bodies that forms cartilage, ligaments, tendons, and connective tissue. Vitamin C is an essential antioxidant, which boosts the immune system and aids in the healing of wounds. It also increases iron absorption, promotes healthy gums, and can help prevent numerous diseases. It can be found in tomatoes, cauliflower, peas, broccoli, potatoes, green beans, carrots, sweet red peppers, parsnips, squash, cantaloupe, avocados, bananas, strawberries, apples, pears, mangos, raspberries, apricots, peaches, plums, cherries, watermelon, kiwi, strawberries, pineapple, blackberries, blueberries, and soybeans.

Minerals   Each and every cell in our bodies contains minerals. They help your baby's body to function properly. Minerals are broken up into two categories—major and trace. Major minerals are needed in larger quantities while trace minerals are needed in smaller amounts, but are no less important for your baby's development.

Major Minerals

Calcium – Essential in building strong bones, and teeth, the stronger your baby's bones grow now means the stronger they'll be in adulthood. Calcium is also important for heartbeat regulation, blood clotting, and muscle function. It can be found in cheese, yogurt, tofu, cottage cheese, soybeans, chickpeas, black beans, lima beans, broccoli, sweet potato, dried apricots, prunes, brown rice, amaranth, and barley.

Magnesium – Helps to build strong bones and teeth. It aids in energy production and is also vital for proper functioning of the immune, nervous, and muscular systems. Magnesium can be found in soybeans, lentils, lima beans, chickpeas, black beans, fish, pork, lamb, beef, parsnips, corn, butternut squash, sweet potatoes, beets, eggplant, peas, potatoes, avocados, bananas, apricots, prunes, tofu, millet, brown rice, barley, amaranth, oats, and quinoa.

Phosphorous – Works with calcium to help build strong bones and teeth. It can be found in yogurt, corn, parsnips, peas, potatoes, prunes, kiwi, lima beans, fish, pork, red meat, poultry, soybeans, lentils, chickpeas, black beans, eggs, quinoa, brown rice, amaranth, barley, oats, and millet.

Potassium – Essential electrolyte that works together with sodium to help regulate blood pressure and maintain water balance in the body. Also aids in nerve, kidney, and muscle functions. It can be found in bananas, cantaloupe, apricots, prunes, peaches, plums, cherries, avocados, strawberries, kiwi, blackberries, cauliflower, tomatoes, corn, squash, peas, potatoes, carrots, beets, parsnips, sweet potato, lima beans, soybeans, lentils, chickpeas, black beans, fish, meat, poultry, amaranth, quinoa, and eggs.

Sodium – Essential electrolyte that works together with potassium to help regulate blood pressure and maintain water balance in the body. Also aids in nerve, kidney, and muscle functions. While too little sodium can throw off the body's balance, too much is also bad, as it can stress your baby's kidneys and may even slow her growth. Avoid adding salt to your baby's food—let her get what she needs from naturally occurring sodium.

The ABC's of Good Nutrition

It can be found in fish, meat, poultry, soybeans, lima beans, chickpeas, sweet potatoes, broccoli, squash, corn, cauliflower, leeks, beets, spinach, parsnips, carrots, potatoes, and eggs.

••

Trace Minerals

Iron – Produces hemoglobin, which is critically important in the production of red blood cells, which are vital in delivering oxygen to the brain and all cells in the body. Iron also helps with energy production. Your baby is born with a store of iron for the first 6 months. After that, you will need to make sure he gets the iron he needs from his diet, which is mainly breast milk or formula for the first year. Because infants are at a higher risk of an iron deficiency, be sure to discuss your child's iron needs with his pediatrician—supplement drops may be recommended. Iron can be found in breast milk, fortified infant formula, fortified baby cereals, dried prunes, dried apricots, lima beans, asparagus, spinach, beets, leeks, peas, potatoes, soybeans, lentils, chickpeas, black beans, pork, red meat, tofu, quinoa, barley, and amaranth.

Copper – Helps produce hemoglobin, which is essential to red blood cells. Copper also aids in the formation of collagen, which is vital to all body tissues. Copper can be found in pork, red meat, soybeans, lentils, chickpeas, black beans, lima beans, tofu, squash, peas, carrots, potatoes, asparagus, sweet potatoes, parsnips, avocados, bananas, pears, apples, blackberries, pineapple, kiwi, peaches, prunes, apricots, mangoes, barley, quinoa, brown rice, amaranth, and millet.

Manganese – Helps with blood sugar regulation, energy metabolism, and nervous system function. It can be found in raspberries, prunes, kiwi, pineapple, blackberries, blueberries, avocados, bananas, lima beans, asparagus, spinach, beets, leeks, eggplant, sweet potatoes, parsnips, squash, peas, potatoes, carrots, soybeans, corn, tomatoes, squash, broccoli, lentils, chickpeas, black beans, barley, oats, millet, amaranth, quinoa, and brown rice.

Selenium – An immune system booster that works together with Vitamin E, as an antioxidant to protect cells from damage and disease, including cancer, asthma, and heart disease. It can be found in fish, pork, red meat, poultry, lentils, chickpeas, lima beans, eggs, oats, barley, quinoa, and amaranth.

Zinc – Helps in the healing of wounds by promoting cell growth and boosts the immune system by helping to ward off infection. Zinc also helps with your baby's vision, sense of smell, and taste. It can be found in ginger, oats, avocados, peaches, blackberries, lima beans, asparagus, parsnips, peas, potatoes, soybeans, lentils, chickpeas, black beans, pork, red meat, millet, barley, amaranth, brown rice, and quinoa.

• •

Protein

Protein is the building material of the body. It is used to construct and maintain cells, muscles, tendons, organs, hair, and nails. It also aids in tissue repair, protection from infection, and is a good source of energy. Babies need more protein relative to body size than adults because they are growing so fast. Protein can be found in breast milk, formula, eggs, fish, meat, poultry, soybeans, lentils, chickpeas, black beans, lima beans, peas, corn, potatoes, prunes, cheese, yogurt, tofu, cottage cheese, brown rice, amaranth, barley, millet, and quinoa.

• •

Fat

Good Fat

The good fats are monounsaturated, polyunsaturated, and omega-3 (DHA) fatty acids. Saturated fats, while not so great for adults, are necessary, in moderation, for babies. These fats help fuel your baby's reserve energy, help the body use vitamins, and aid in the manufacturing of hormones. Good fats are also essential for brain development, nerves, and myelin (the nerve coating in the brain). Healthy fats are critically important to your growing baby and should make up about 40% of her calories. Avoid giving your baby reduced-fat or low-fat foods until age 2. These good fats can be found in breast milk, formula, avocados, red meat, olive oil, cheese, nuts, tofu, and salmon.

The ABC's of Good Nutrition

Fat
(Continued)

Bad Fat

The bad fats are trans-fats, often labeled "hydrogenated". Too much bad fat raises blood cholesterol and can result in inflammatory diseases, such as heart disease and arthritis, as well as asthma and eczema. Trans-fats are found in processed and manufactured foods such as potato chips, frozen pizzas, "fast foods", and margarine. Avoid feeding your child any processed food until he is at least 2 years old. These foods are full of empty calories and, with childhood obesity on the rise, it's best to stay away from them as much as you can.

• •

Dietary Fiber

Helps the digestive system function properly and prevents constipation. Fiber also regulates the amount of cholesterol in the blood. However, it is important not to give your baby too much fiber as this could cause an upset stomach or diarrhea, and interfere with the absorption of minerals. Dietary fiber can be found in soybeans, chickpeas, lentils, black beans, mangoes, apples, pears, apricots, prunes, bananas, avocados, peaches, cherries, kiwi, pineapple, blackberries, raspberries, strawberries, blueberries, cauliflower, lima beans, sweet red peppers, potatoes, carrots, beets, peas, eggplant, sweet potatoes, parsnips, brown rice, amaranth, barley, millet, oats, and quinoa.

• •

Carbohydrates

Carbohydrates are the body's main source of energy. They are broken into two groups—simple and complex.

Complex = good carbohydrates. They stay in your baby's system longer than simple carbohydrates and come from whole foods, not sugars. They give your baby the energy he needs for all of the growing he has to do. Good sources of complex carbohydrates are brown rice, amaranth, millet, oats, barley, quinoa, whole grain pastas, beans, fruits, and vegetables.

Simple = not so good carbohydrates. They are digested quickly, leaving your baby with minimal energy. Simple carbohydrates are basically empty calories such as sugar, corn syrup, and processed sweets. They should be avoided or only given sporadically. It's better for your baby to get his energy from the goodness of whole foods. He'll have more energy and will be less irritable.

• •

Antioxidants It is widely believed that antioxidants play an important role in helping to ward off heart disease, cancer, and numerous other diseases, by protecting cells from damage caused by free radicals. The antioxidant levels in whole foods are greater than the levels found in antioxidant supplements or vitamins. According to the USDA, the top 20 antioxidant-rich foods are:

1. Small Red Beans
2. Wild Blueberries
3. Red Kidney Beans
4. Pinto Beans
5. Farmed Blueberries
6. Cranberries
7. Artichokes (cooked)
8. Blackberries
9. Prunes
10. Raspberries
11. Strawberries
12. Red Delicious Apples
13. Granny Smith Apples
14. Pecans
15. Sweet Cherries
16. Black Plums
17. Russet Potatoes (cooked)
18. Black Beans
19. Plums
20. Gala Apples

Other foods that contain antioxidants are: pineapples, kiwi, bell peppers, spinach, beets, dried apricots, soybeans, barley, millet, oats, cinnamon, oregano, ginger and turmeric.

Special Diets

Vegetarian
A vegetarian diet can be loaded with health benefits such as a decreased risk of cancer, diabetes, and obesity. It has also been shown that children fed a vegetarian diet are less likely to have allergies and gastrointestinal problems. However, if you wish to feed your baby a vegetarian diet, you will need to work with her pediatrician to make sure she is getting the nutrition she needs. It is particularly important that she gets enough iron, protein, fat, calcium, and vitamin B12.

Iron – a diet lacking in iron can cause your baby to feel weak or tired and can even cause her to become anemic. Foods like lentils, beans, oats, spinach, broccoli, and soy are good sources of iron.

Protein – is one of the building blocks for your baby's growth. Babies need a lot of protein to keep up with how fast they are growing. Protein can be found in breast milk and formula; other sources include chickpeas, beans, soy, grains and select fruits, and vegetables.

Fat – your baby should be getting about 40% of her calories from healthy fats. Healthy fats are critical to brain and nervous system development. In addition to breast milk and formula, healthy fats can be found in avocado, olive oil, and coconut.

Calcium – if your baby doesn't get enough calcium, her teeth and bones can become weak. A calcium deficiency may even stunt her growth. In addition to breast milk and formula, calcium can be found in broccoli, sweet potatoes, and beans.

Vitamin B12 – a deficiency of this vitamin is not good for the nervous system and can cause anemia. Vegetarians often need a vitamin B12 supplement, because it is only found in breast milk, formula, and animal products.

 Always check with your baby's pediatrician before giving any kind of supplement.

Vegan and Macrobiotic
The American Academy of Pediatrics does not recommend feeding your baby a vegan or macrobiotic diet. These diets are far too restrictive to meet your baby's needs. They do not contain enough vitamins, nutrients, energy, and minerals that are essential for a baby's normal growth and development. Feeding your baby a vegan or macrobiotic diet could result in failure to thrive.

Preemies

My second son, Brendan, arrived two months premature and spent 6 weeks in the Neonatal Intensive Care Unit. Having a child who had to fight for his life and whom we nearly lost, was a life-altering experience that I will never forget. It has brought the topic of preemies and their care extremely close to my heart. Bringing a preemie home is a much different experience than bringing home a full term, healthy baby. I am sure many of you know what I'm talking about.

With my first son, Royce, everything was happy, easy, and as it should be. Milestones came naturally and when it was time to start on solids, at 5 months, we just did with no worries. With Brendan, we were overwhelmed with worry, doctor's appointments, mixing breast milk with special formula, and handling him with such extra care that the thought of starting on solids seemed a million years away. It wasn't until an appointment with one of Brendan's primary doctors when he was 5 months old (from his birth date, not due date) that my eyes were opened.

The doctor asked me when I planned to start Brendan on solids. I told him I hadn't even thought about it. He told me that it was time. I looked at him cross-eyed and said I was scared to change our routine—what if something happened? He said that Brendan was stable, putting on weight, and, while he still had a lot of catching up to do, he was otherwise healthy. He told me not to be afraid. He said that most preemies have such an intense start to their lives that the simple pleasure of a homemade meal can do wonders. I was sold. As soon as we got home, I mashed a banana and mixed it with some warm breast milk and rice cereal. The doctor was right. Not only did Brendan take to swallowing solid food immediately; he ate the entire 4 oz meal! I was completely shocked. He was so happy eating and turned out to have quite an appetite for such a little guy. That was a real turning point for both of us. The best part is that Brendan began to thrive in a way I hadn't seen before.

Preemies need the very best and most complete nutrition available, because they have so much catching up to do, and many have medical issues beyond just putting on weight. As parents of preemies, we should not underestimate the power of a healthy diet and delicious food.

✳ Every preemie is different, not only developmentally, but medically as well. It is of the utmost importance that you consult your preemie's doctor(s) before starting him on solids or straying from his normal routine in any way.

Herbs and Spices

Herbs and spices can enhance the flavor and aroma of any meal. Use them in a way that works into your life, culture, and diet. Do not be afraid to use them, but also don't feel pressured to use them. Introduce herbs and spices one at a time, just as you would individual foods, to see if your child has any reactions. If you have a family history of food allergies or intolerances, please check with your pediatrician before introducing any herbs or spices to your baby's diet.

When shopping for dried herbs and spices, buy organic whenever possible, they are less likely to have been irradiated. Most dried herbs and spices on the market, unless otherwise specified, have gone through an ionized radiation process. While this process kills bacteria and increases shelf life, it lessens the health benefits of the herb or spice and may even pose a health risk due to the radiation.

Herbs

You can use fresh or dried herbs in your homemade baby food. While dried herbs are a little more convenient, because they can be stocked in your pantry for 6 months, I prefer to use fresh herbs. I feel they taste better than dried. Dry herbs are more potent than fresh. When using dried herbs start with a pinch—you can always add more. Fresh herbs are available in most grocery stores and will stay fresh, wrapped in a damp paper towel in the refrigerator, for about one week.

Basil – A light, fresh, almost mint-like flavor. There are many different varieties of basil, with sweet basil being the most popular and available. Basil contains flavonoids, which protect the body's cell structures from free radical damage, thereby giving it anti-cancer benefits. Basil can be found, both fresh and dried, in most grocery stores. When buying fresh, look for bright green leaves. It pairs well with tomatoes, squash, fish, and pasta.

Cilantro – Slightly stronger, more aromatic flavor than Italian flat-leaf parsley, which it resembles. Cilantro is actually fresh coriander. It has been known to have anti-inflammatory and antimicrobial properties. Cilantro has also been shown to have cholesterol-lowering effects. When buying cilantro, look for a rich, deep green color. It pairs well with avocados, black beans, tomatoes, corn, bell pepper, mangoes, and chicken.

Mint – Has a fresh, cool, and sometimes sweet flavor. There are roughly 25 different varieties of mint, with peppermint and spearmint being the most widely used and available. Mint has long been known to be a digestive aid and peppermint, specifically, contains limonene, which has been shown to provide protection from some forms of cancer. Mint is widely available both fresh and dried; however, fresh mint really tastes better. When buying fresh mint, look for bright green leaves. It pairs well with peas, lamb, corn, asparagus, green beans, and eggplant.

Oregano – Has more of a strong, earthy flavor. It is known for its antimicrobial and antioxidant properties. According to the USDA, oregano has the highest antioxidant level found in any herb and more than in most other antioxidant-rich foods. When buying fresh oregano, look for it to have a strong green color. It pairs well with tomatoes, tomato sauce, pasta, mushrooms, eggs, squash, and poultry.

Parsley – Has a fragrant, crisp flavor and is not bitter. Parsley is a nutrient-rich herb. It is full of iron, vitamin C, folate, potassium, magnesium, zinc, and calcium. It also contains the anti-cancer compound limonene. When buying fresh parsley, look for the Italian flat-leaf variety, not the curly variety. It should be bright green in color and not wilted. It pairs well with meats, poultry, grains, carrots, parsnips, potatoes, and stock.

Rosemary – Has a strong piney and woody flavor. Rosemary is high in antioxidants, has anti-inflammatory properties, can help improve digestion and has been shown to increase blood flow to the brain. When buying fresh rosemary, look for sprigs with deep green-colored leaves. It pairs well with beef, poultry, lamb, butternut squash, pumpkin, potatoes, and eggs.

Sage – Has a minty, earthy, and slightly bitter flavor. Sage has been shown to boost the immune system and improve circulation. It is also known to dry up the milk in lactating women, so if you are nursing or pumping, avoid eating sage. Fresh sage should have rich silvery-green leaves. It pairs well with butternut squash, pumpkin, beans, pork, and poultry.

Herbs and Spices

Tarragon – Has a peppery, almost licorice flavor. Tarragon is rich in anti-inflammatory and anti-cancer compounds. When buying fresh tarragon, look for sprigs that are firm and straight, with green leaves. It pairs well with poultry, lamb, fish, potatoes, carrots, cauliflower, asparagus, tomatoes, and broccoli.

Thyme – Has a lemony, slightly minty flavor. It is high in antioxidants and may have anti-inflammatory benefits as well. When buying fresh thyme, look for sprigs with small, dark grayish-green leaves. It pairs well with poultry, pork, beef, lamb, fish, black beans, stock, potatoes, and carrots.

Spices

Spices are not only convenient to use—they will also make your kitchen smell incredibly appetizing. Spices can be stocked in your pantry and will stay fresh for 6 months, when stored in an airtight container.

Cinnamon – Has an aromatic, sweet, and light spicy flavor. There are over 200 different varieties of cinnamon, with Ceylon being the most popular and widely available in grocery stores. In addition to its high antioxidant levels, cinnamon has also been shown to aid in circulation and digestion. It is available in sticks or already ground. Cinnamon is my favorite spice; it is easy to use and tastes great with a large variety of foods. It pairs well with fruit, sweet potatoes, pumpkin, eggplant, parsnips, and oatmeal.

Curry – Aromatic and gingery in flavor. Curry is a blend of many different spices—turmeric, cardamom, and cinnamon to name a few. Each spice adds its own unique taste and health benefit. Stick to mild curry for the first year. It pairs well with lamb, chicken, hearty vegetables, and rice.

Garlic – When cooked, garlic is delightfully aromatic with a mildly spicy taste. Garlic has been touted for its health benefits for centuries. It is full of vitamins and minerals and has been shown to help ward off heart disease, fight infection, lower blood pressure, and possibly aid in fighting off some forms of cancer. It pairs well with most vegetables, especially broccoli and tomatoes, pasta, poultry, meat, and fish.

Ginger – Fragrant, with a slightly sweet and hot flavor. There are many different varieties of ginger. Jamaican ginger is the most common. It is well known to provide relief from gastrointestinal ailments and can be helpful when your baby has gas, an upset stomach, or suffers from motion sickness. Ginger is widely available both fresh and dried. Avoid pickled ginger, as it is full of sodium. Fresh ginger should be firm to the touch and have smooth skin. Un-peeled fresh ginger will stay fresh in your refrigerator for about 2 weeks. It pairs well with fruit, carrots, pumpkin, butternut squash, parsnips, sweet potatoes, broccoli, rice, poultry, and meat.

Nutmeg – Warm, sweet, yet strong flavor. A little nutmeg goes a long way. Nutmeg has properties that can be helpful when your baby has diarrhea. It pairs well with fruit, sweet potatoes, parsnips, butternut squash, pumpkin, and carrots.

Turmeric – Warm, earthy, and a little bitter in flavor. Turmeric is known to have anti-inflammatory properties and can be helpful when your baby has gas or swollen gums from teething. Turmeric has also been shown to decrease pain from rheumatoid arthritis. Additionally, it is a powerful antioxidant that can help protect against childhood cancers, including leukemia. It pairs well with beef, lamb, lentils, and rice.

Foods to Avoid

No honey until 12 months
It can contain botulism spores that your baby's immature immune system can't fight off.

No cow's milk until 12 months
It contains casein, which is a known allergen.

No soy cheese until 12 months
Most brands contain casein.

No chocolate until 12 months
Chocolate contains caffeine and is also an allergen. Chocolate makes a great treat for your child's first birthday!

No whole wheat until 12 months
Whole wheat is an allergen.

No added sugar or salt until at least 12 months
Let your baby enjoy the taste of food in its natural state.

No processed or fried food until at least 12 months
Whenever possible, avoid giving these kinds of food to your children. They are one of the primary causes of childhood obesity.

No Peanuts, Seeds or Tree Nuts (Walnuts, Pecans, etc.) until given the okay from your child's pediatrician
When to introduce these foods is currently being widely debated, due to the steady increase of food allergies in children. Please consult with your pediatrician before introducing.

No artificial sweeteners
It is best to avoid giving these to your child (and yourself) as much as possible. Artificial sweeteners are known carcinogens.

No low-fat or fat-free foods
Your baby's brain is growing until age 2 and healthy fat is essential for proper brain and nervous system growth.

Avoid deli meats and hot dogs preserved with nitrates or nitrites

Nitrates and nitrites are often used to preserve cured meats and hot dogs. Unfortunately, when cooked, these preservatives are known to be carcinogenic. It is especially important for pregnant women and young children to avoid these preservatives.

Avoid giving your child juice until 12 months

It is full of sugar and will fill her up with empty calories, not to mention that too much sugar is not good for her teeth. When giving your child juice, dilute it with purified water. Infused waters are a terrific juice alternative; they have no added sugar, but do have the extra flavor that babies and toddlers love. See page 208 for my deliciously refreshing infused water recipes.

No unpasteurized soft cheeses until 12–18 months

They put your child (and pregnant women) at risk for listeria poisoning. These cheeses include: Blue cheese, Roquefort, Mexican cheeses, Camembert, Brie, Feta, and Goat Cheese.

No raw sprouts for babies or young children

They are often contaminated with Salmonella, E. Coli, and Canavanine toxins.

No fish containing high levels of mercury

Avoid giving your child and yourself (especially if you are pregnant) these fish altogether. Currently they include: Swordfish, Tuna (including canned tuna), King Mackerel, Marlin, Bluefish, and Chilean Sea Bass, among others. Mercury poisoning is very dangerous and can cause delayed development, heart damage, mental retardation, and nerve disorders. For the most up-to-date information on safe fish go to the Environmental Defense Fund's site at www.edf.org/seafoodhealth.

No raw fish until at least 2 years

Raw fish are known to carry parasites.

No shellfish until at least 2 years

Shellfish are highly allergenic.

 If you have a family history of food allergies, be sure to consult with your child's pediatrician before introducing any foods of concern.

Choking 911
For infants 12 months and under

* If you think your baby is choking, but she is able to cough, allow her to keep coughing until she clears what is in her throat.

* However, if your baby's face suddenly turns blue or red and he can't cough or cry, he could have something lodged in his throat. Call 911 and begin back and chest thrusts immediately. If someone is there with you, have them call 911; if you are alone, put the phone on speaker or hold it to your ear with your shoulder, but at no time should emergency care be stopped to make a phone call.

* Place your baby face-down on your forearm and gently support her head and neck with the palm of your hand. Rest your forearm on the top of your thigh, so the baby's head is lower than her body. Give 5 back thrusts with the heel of your hand in a firm but fluid forward motion between the shoulder blades.

* After 5 back thrusts, if your baby isn't coughing yet, turn him face-up on your forearm, with your hand cradling his head. Place your arm on top of your thigh and make sure the baby's head is lower than his body. Begin 5 chest thrusts by placing the pads of 3 fingers on the chest, in between the nipples, and pushing straight down about 1". Allow the chest to rise back up before beginning another thrust. Repeat 5 back thrusts with 5 chest thrusts until your baby starts coughing.

* If your baby still isn't coughing or loses consciousness, begin infant CPR (see other side).

* Other causes of a closed airway could be an allergic reaction, illness, or infection—whatever the cause, 911 should be called immediately.

Infant CPR
For infants 12 months and under

* If your baby is unconscious and not breathing, call 911 while beginning CPR immediately.

* Place the baby on a FIRM surface (not on a crib, bed, changing table or piece of furniture).

* Try to open the baby's airway by tilting her head back and opening her mouth, by gently lifting her chin. Take a quick 5–10 seconds to see if the baby is breathing, by getting down low and looking to see if her chest is rising and falling, or if you feel breath coming out of her mouth.

* If the baby isn't breathing, cover both his nose and mouth with your mouth and give 2 quick, but soft breaths—just enough to make his chest rise (babies have small lungs and don't need a ton of air to fill them). Be sure to pause between rescue breaths, in order to allow for the air to escape from the lungs, prior to initiating a second rescue breath.

* If you don't see the baby's chest rising and falling, the airway could be blocked, and you should immediately begin back and chest thrusts (see other side).

* After the 2 breaths, place 2 fingers together in the middle of the baby's chest, just below the nipples. Pushing straight down, give 30 quick, but smooth chest compressions. Your fingers should not compress the baby's chest any more than 1 inch.

* Continue to repeat 2 breaths, with 30 chest compressions, until help arrives. Do not stop CPR at any time, unless the baby starts breathing on her own.

* Be sure that you and your children's caregivers, grandparents, and anyone who will be responsible for taking care of your children all know Choking 911 and Infant CPR. Check with the American Red Cross (www.Americanredcross.org) for more information.

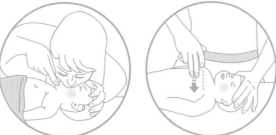

LET'S GET STARTED

Tools

You don't need fancy equipment to make your own baby food—you probably have these things in your kitchen already!

* Vegetable peeler
* Strainer/colander
* Cutting board
* Sharp knife
* Wooden spoon
* Pot, with steamer basket and lid
* Oven mitts
* Skillet
* Baking sheet
* Unbleached parchment paper
* Immersion blender and food processor
* Fork
* Heavy-duty glass bowl or stainless steel bowl
* Spatula
* Small saucepan

Shopping

Fruit and vegetables

Look for fresh fruit that is ripe and bruise-free. When making baby food, try to always use ripe fruit—it allows for the best taste and texture. Let under-ripe fruit ripen on your counter for a few days before preparing. Most fresh fruits can be stored at room temperature, with the exception of berries, which should be stored in a plastic bag or container in the refrigerator. Frozen fruit can also be used to make baby food, especially if you want to prepare an out of season variety. Avoid canned fruit; it is usually full of extra sugar and syrup.

Fresh vegetables should be colorful, firm, and crisp. Avoid vegetables that look wilted or are browning. Most vegetables can be stored in a plastic bag in the refrigerator. However, potatoes, sweet potatoes, and squash can be stored at room temperature on your counter. Frozen vegetables are also a good choice, because they are frozen at the peak of freshness and can save you some prep time. I particularly like using frozen peas, because they don't need to be de-shelled. Avoid canned vegetables; they often contain added sodium.

Whenever possible, buy produce that was grown in the USA. We have stricter guidelines for farming than many other countries.

Poultry and Pork

Pork, chicken, and turkey are naturally lean and are great sources of protein and iron. Free range chicken even contains DHA, an essential building block of healthy brain tissue. Look for pork and poultry that are fresh and have a nice pink color. Avoid any pork or poultry that has an off-smell or looks gray. Be sure to double-check the expiration dates.

Pork can be purchased either ground, in chops, or as a tenderloin. Poultry can be purchased either ground or in whole pieces. If there is no prepackaged ground meat available, you can ask the butcher to grind some for you. Whenever possible, look for pork, chicken, and turkey that have not been treated with hormones, steroids, or antibiotics.

Unprepared poultry and pork should be wrapped tightly or stored in an airtight container. It will stay fresh in the refrigerator for up to 3 days and up to 3 months in the freezer. Allow frozen poultry and pork to thaw in the refrigerator—never on your counter. Pork and poultry should go into the refrigerator or freezer as soon as you get home to prevent the growth of bacteria.

Shopping

Beef and Lamb

When shopping for red meat, like beef or lamb, look for leaner cuts that are firm and have a rich red color. Avoid meat that is gray or very fatty. While beef and lamb are rich in iron and protein, they can also be high in cholesterol. It is best to limit red meat servings to 1–2 times per week. Whenever possible, look for meat that has not been treated with hormones, steroids, or antibiotics. Additionally, beef that has been grass-fed contains DHA. Beef can be purchased either ground or in whole pieces, such as a chop or filet. If there is no pre-packaged ground meat available, you can ask the butcher to grind some for you. Lamb can be purchased as a chop or steak.

It's a good idea to double check the expiration dates on all meat before purchasing, to make sure you are getting the freshest available. Unprepared beef and lamb should be wrapped tightly or stored in an airtight container. The meat will stay fresh in the refrigerator for up to 3 days and up to 3 months in the freezer. Allow frozen meat to thaw in the refrigerator—never on the counter. Beef and lamb should go into the refrigerator or freezer as soon as you get home to prevent bacteria from growing.

Fish

Fish, especially wild caught Alaskan salmon, is a fantastic source of omega 3's (DHA), which are essential for your baby's developing brain. Avoid fish that contain high levels of mercury, like swordfish and tuna. Mercury is especially harmful for babies, children, and pregnant women. **Too much mercury can cause learning disabilities in children, autoimmune disease, and even heart problems.** Wild salmon has some of the lowest levels of mercury. It also has the highest levels of beneficial omega-3 fatty acids, making it a great choice for your baby. It can be purchased in filets, by the pound, or whole.

If desired, you can ask the fishmonger to trim off the skin or de-bone and filet a whole fish for you. Put the fish directly into your refrigerator or freezer when you get home. It should be wrapped tightly or stored in an airtight container. Unprepared fish will stay fresh in the refrigerator for up to 3 days and up to 3 months in the freezer. Allow frozen fish to thaw in the refrigerator, never on the counter. Visit **www.edf.org/seafoodhealth** for more info on mercury levels in fish.

Preparation

The most important thing when preparing food for your baby is cleanliness. Be sure your hands, prep area, utensils, and cutting boards are clean and sanitized before each use. Cutting boards, in particular, are a breeding ground for bacteria. It's a good idea to have separate cutting boards, one for meat, poultry, and fish and another for produce. While wood cutting boards are okay for fruit and vegetables, I highly recommend using a dishwasher-safe board for meat, poultry, and fish preparation, so it can be properly cleaned and disinfected.

Fruit and Vegetables Wash all fruit and vegetables thoroughly under cold running water, even if they are organic. With the exception of berries, all fruit needs to be peeled. For vegetables, it varies; some need to be peeled, like carrots, parsnips, and beets; some just need to be rinsed, like cauliflower, broccoli, and spinach; others just need to be cut in half and placed in the oven, like butternut squash, eggplant, and pumpkin.

Meat, Poultry, and Fish When you are working with raw meat, poultry, and fish it is very important to prevent the spread of bacteria. Wash your hands thoroughly and repeatedly with soap and water when working with these foods. As an extra precaution, rinse raw poultry under cold running water before preparing to get rid of excess bacteria and germs.

The best thing about baby food preparation? You don't need to worry about exact measurements and perfect chopping skills, because everything is getting pureed!

* Always keep knives and other sharp objects out of children's reach.

Cooking

Fruit and Vegetables

The best way to cook fruits and vegetables for your baby is to lightly steam them. Food can retain most of its nutrients during the steaming process, because it doesn't come into direct contact with the cooking water. To steam, pour enough water into a medium or large pot so that it is about 1 inch deep. Bring to a boil over high heat and place the prepared fruit or vegetable into a steamer basket. Put the steamer basket into the pot and cover with a tight-fitting lid. Steam as directed in the recipe. Make sure the cooking water does not touch the bottom of the basket.

When steaming foods that take a little longer to cook, like sweet potatoes, it's a good idea to monitor the water level occasionally. If the water boils off, the bottom of the pot will burn—I learned this the hard way. If the water level looks too low, just add more as needed.

Another great cooking option is roasting. Roasting is particularly good for hearty vegetables like butternut squash, sweet potato, potato, and pumpkin. As with steaming, foods that are roasted are able to hold on to most of their nutrients. Roasting brings out the natural sweetness of these vegetables and they taste absolutely delicious. Roasting takes longer than steaming but requires very little effort, because the oven does all the work, and the result is definitely worth the wait.

There are some cooking methods that I do not recommend. Boiling fruits and vegetables, for example, kills the most vitamins and nutrients, because food is cooked directly in the water. The longer food is cooked in water, the more nutrients, taste, and texture are boiled off. Fruits and veggies can lose up to 50% of their vitamins, nutrients, and antioxidants during the boiling process. Microwaving is also not recommended because it can cook unevenly and there is some debate as to the possible negative health effects associated with microwave cooking. Frying is absolutely not recommended as a way to cook baby food.

✳ To avoid burning your hands, always use an oven mitt when handling hot pots, pans, baking sheets, and roasting pans.

Cooking

Meat, Poultry, and Fish

It is extremely important to make sure that the meat, poultry, and fish you prepare for your baby are cooked thoroughly. The two best ways to cook these foods for your baby are poaching and roasting.

To poach ground meat or poultry, pour enough water or stock into a medium skillet so the liquid level is about ½ inch deep. Bring the liquid to a boil over medium–high heat and add the meat or poultry. Let it cook for 3–5 minutes until cooked through. During the cooking process, frequently break up the meat or poultry with the end of a spatula. This way, it will stay in nice small pieces. Once the meat is cooked, remove it from the skillet with a slotted spoon and place into a food processor in preparation for pureeing. Reserve the cooking liquid to add while pureeing.

The poaching process is basically the same with fish. Pour enough water or stock into a skillet so it measures measures ½–1" deep depending on the thickness of the fish filet. Let the liquid come to a boil over medium–high heat. Add the fish filet and let it cook for about 3 minutes; then turn it over with a spatula and let cook for 2–3 minutes more. You'll know the fish is cooked when it is opaque all the way through. Remove the fish filet from the skillet with a spatula and place into a bowl. Fish is very tender when cooked and does not need to be pureed; it can simply be mashed with the back of a fork.

Roasting is a great way to cook whole pieces of meat or poultry, such as chops, steaks, filets, breasts, and thighs. Fish filets are also delicious when roasted. It takes a little longer, but allows the meat, poultry, and fish to remain moist and juicy. Preheat the oven as per the recipe's instructions and line a baking sheet with unbleached parchment paper. Place the meat, poultry or fish on the parchment paper and roast as directed in the recipe. Once cooked, remove it from the oven and let cool for about 5 minutes. Fish can easily be flaked and mashed with the back of a fork. Meat and poultry should be cut into cubes and placed in a food processor, in preparation for pureeing.

✳ To avoid burning your hand, always use an oven mitt when handling hot pots, pans, roasting dishes, and baking sheets.

Pureeing

Before pureeing, make sure your immersion blender and food processor are clean and sanitized. Add cooking water, breast milk, formula, or stock, as needed, to thin purees, and add baby cereals, as needed, to thicken purees. Some purees, like banana, avocado, potatoes, and fish, can simply be mashed with the back of a fork.

Food Processor

The food processor will puree just about anything and is ideal for pureeing pasty foods like beans, meat, and poultry, as well as fruit and veggies. Place the desired food into the bowl of the food processor, place the lid with hand motor securely on top, and pulse until the desired consistency and texture of the food is achieved. Scrape the sides of the food processor bowl with a spoon or spatula in between pulses, if needed. The food processor is also great for making food when you are away from home.

* The food processor is meant to be used with a pulsing motion. Holding the button down in a continuous manner, for longer than 15 seconds, may overheat the motor.

Immersion Blender

The immersion blender works best with soft foods, like ripe fruits and cooked vegetables. It is ideal for making large batches of staple foods like apples and butternut squash. However, it is versatile enough to make small servings as well. Place the desired food into a heavy duty glass or stainless steel mixing bowl. Work the immersion blender in a circular motion in the bowl until the desired consistency and texture of the food is achieved.

* Avoid trying to blend anything pasty, like potatoes, meat, poultry, or beans, with an immersion blender as it may jam the motor.

* Immersion blenders are meant to be used with a pulsing motion. Holding down the button of an immersion blender for more than about 15 seconds, continuously, may overheat the motor.

✳ Always keep immersion blender and food processor out of children's reach.

Serving

Place the desired amount of puree in a small serving bowl and check to make sure the consistency and temperature are what your baby can handle. The best place to feed your baby is in a clean high chair, safely strapped in, and with a soft tipped spoon.

Spoons carry bacteria from saliva while feeding. Do not serve leftovers from a bowl or jar that your baby has already eaten from. To avoid waste, try serving a smaller amount in a separate bowl—you can always add more.

Fruit purees taste great served cool, warm, or at room temperature. Most veggie purees taste best warm, but can be served cool as well. Meat, poultry, and fish purees need to be served warm. Always check to make sure your baby's food is neither too cool nor too warm.

To warm the puree before serving, place the desired amount in a small saucepan and warm over medium–low heat for 1–2 minutes, stirring frequently. You can also warm your baby's food in a bottle warmer. Place the Sage Spoonfuls jar into the bottle warmer and warm to the desired temperature. You can even feed directly from the jar. This is particularly convenient for mealtimes away from home. I do not recommend heating your baby's food in a microwave. It heats unevenly and can cause hot spots in the food that could possibly burn your child's mouth.

To defrost the contents of your Sage Spoonfuls jar, move the jar from the freezer to the refrigerator a few hours (or overnight) before you intend to serve it. If you are pressed for time, run the jar under hot water for 10 seconds to loosen the puree; then warm the contents in a small saucepan, with a little water, over medium–low heat. Another way to defrost your frozen baby food is to place the jar into a bowl of hot water to just below the cap for 15–20 minutes; then serve cool.

✳ Never leave your baby or child unattended while he is eating, and be aware of foods that pose a choking hazard.

✳ Do not serve your baby any meat, poultry or fish that has been sitting out for more than 1 hour or any fruit, veggie, or bean puree that has been out more than 2 hours.

Storing

In this day and age, we all lead incredibly busy and hectic lives. With Sage Spoonfuls, homemade baby food can be prepared in large batches and stored in the freezer for up to 3 months. It only takes 1 hour every two weeks to keep your freezer stocked with delicious and nutritious food for your baby.

After pureeing your food of choice, it should either be served right away or placed into Sage Spoonfuls jars and put in the refrigerator or freezer. The temperature of your refrigerator should be set between 37–40 degrees Fahrenheit and your freezer should be set between -3 and 0 degrees Fahrenheit. I am a big fan of flash freezing because it ensures the freshness of the food. If you let the food cool to room temperature before freezing, it gives bacteria a chance to grow. To flash freeze, put the puree you want to store into Sage Spoonfuls jars, label the contents, and place directly into the freezer.

When stored in Sage Spoonfuls jars, most purees will stay fresh for up to 3 days in the refrigerator and up to 3 months in the freezer. Make sure to label and date the contents before storing. Date them again when moving the jars from the freezer to the refrigerator.

When you are ready to serve a puree that has been in the freezer, move the jar to the refrigerator and allow it to thaw for a few hours or overnight. If you are pressed for time, run the jar under hot water for 10 seconds to loosen the puree; then warm it in a small saucepan, with a little water, over medium–low heat. You can also defrost by placing the jar in a bowl of hot water for 15–20 minutes.

Making Yummy Combinations

One of the many benefits of making your own baby food is the endless flavor combinations. With store bought baby food, we are limited to what the manufacturer thinks are the most popular food combinations. Your baby's taste buds and palate are developing during his first year; it is important to introduce him to as many new tastes and textures as you can.

It is really easy to make yummy combinations. There is no need for exact measurements or detailed recipes; simply combine equal portions of each puree and see what tastes good to you and what flavor combinations your baby likes. For example, if you want to make an apple/pear combo, mix 2 ounces of apple puree with 2 ounces of pear puree. It's that easy.

You can prepare yummy combinations in 2 different ways:

1) Prepare and store each puree, individually, and combine right before serving. For example, make a batch of apple puree and store. Make a batch of pear puree and store. Before serving, scoop out equal portions of apple and pear from their jars and combine in a serving bowl.

Or...

2) Combine purees immediately after preparing and store in Sage Spoonfuls jars. This way they are pre-mixed in the jar and ready to go. For example, make a batch of apple puree and a batch of pear puree. Combine the two purees in a bowl, place into Sage Spoonfuls jars, and store. You can even steam and puree the 2 fruits together, instead of cooking each, individually, first.

This book offers hundreds of yummy combinations that are not only great for your baby's first year, but are also delicious for older babies and toddlers. All you have to do is adjust the portion size and texture.

 Before combining foods, make sure your baby has tried each one, individually, to be sure there are no allergies or food intolerances.

A HOMEMADE LIFESTYLE

Making Mealtime Fun!

Introducing your baby to solids is not only about teaching her to swallow food from a spoon; it also teaches her that mealtime is something to look forward to and enjoy. We all lead very busy lives and kids can easily come to think of eating as a chore, which can lead to picky eaters and bad habits. Taking just a little extra time to make mealtime fun will lay a strong foundation, not only for good nutrition, but for the love of mealtime.

You can start making positive food associations right from the start. Tell your baby what he is eating. Let him touch, smell, and explore the whole fruits and vegetables. He'll love being part of the action.

Leave plenty of time for your baby's meals, especially in the beginning. Be sure not to rush her. If she feels rushed it could attach a negative feeling to mealtime, when it should be something to look forward to.

It's important to avoid putting your personal food aversions onto your baby. My husband has a really strong anti-cheese thing going on—he can't even handle being near it; but most babies and kids love cheese. Every time I give my boys something with cheese, I can see him ready to make a comment and I give him a little wink as a reminder not to say anything.

Mealtime is a great opportunity to bond with your baby. Whenever possible, turn off the TV, put down the cell phone, and avoid the computer. Try listening to music and talking to your baby—even if she can't talk back…yet.

Be a good example. If your baby sees you eating healthy, he will want to eat healthy too!

Keep a camera nearby; you'll be glad you did!

Sage Spoonfuls On-The-Go

With Sage Spoonfuls, leading a homemade lifestyle is easier and more convenient than you may think. Your baby can have healthy, homemade meals on-the-go in nearly any situation, from short outings, to daycare, to overnights and more!

Short Outings, Daytrips, and Daycare
This includes trips to the park, museums, restaurants, doctor's appointments, play dates, birthday parties, amusement parks, shopping, planes, trains, automobiles, daycare, and any other outing that is not over 12 hours long.

Out and About for 1–2 Hours
Fruit, vegetable and bean purees, including those mixed with breast milk, will stay fresh out of the refrigerator for up to 2 hours. Any puree mixed with formula, cheese, yogurt, tofu, meat, poultry, or fish will stay fresh out of the refrigerator for up to 1 hour. Before you leave, pack the Sage Spoonfuls jar in your diaper bag, along with a spoon, bib, and your baby's bottle of breast milk or formula. Breast milk can stay out of refrigeration for up to 4 hours and most formulas can stay out for 1–2 hours. Check the label of your baby's formula to be sure how long it can stay out of the refrigerator.

If you want to serve a warm meal on-the-go, heat the puree to just above your desired temperature, place into Sage Spoonfuls jar, and pack in your diaper bag. Most purees will stay warm in your jar for about an hour.

Out and About for 2–12 Hours
For times when you will be gone longer than 2 hours or need to be away for the day with your baby, the Sage Spoonfuls cooler is perfect. Fruit, vegetable, and bean purees, including those mixed with breast milk or formula, will stay fresh in your cooler, with the frozen ice pack, for up to 12 hours. You can pack the Sage Spoonfuls cooler with a few jars of fresh puree, enough bottles for the day, spoons, bibs, napkins, and even an extra diaper or two.

If you need to leave your baby at daycare, the combination of the Sage Spoonfuls cooler and tote work really well. Pack the cooler with the appropriate number of jars and bottles your child/children will need for the day, along with spoons, bibs, and napkins. The contents of the cooler will stay fresh, with the frozen ice pack, for up to 12 hours, so your child's caregiver won't even need to put your baby's jars and bottles, or sippys in the refrigerator. Everything can stay neatly packed in your cooler.

Sage Spoonfuls On-The-Go

The large tote is great for diapers, blankets, a change of clothes, favorite toy, and a bottle warmer. A bottle warmer not only heats your baby's bottle, but the caregiver can put the Sage Spoonfuls jar in it to warm your baby's meal as well.

Banana puree is especially perfect for any on-the-go feeding situation—it is a no-cook puree and can be prepared fresh in seconds. Just pack a spoon, an empty Sage Spoonfuls jar, and a banana in your diaper bag. When it's time to eat, peel the banana, break it in half, and mash right in the jar with your spoon.

Overnights, Hotels, and Visits to Grandma

This includes vacations, long weekends, staying with friends or relatives, and anything that will take your baby away from home overnight.

If there is a kitchen at your destination

If you are going to spend your time away at the home of a family member, friend, or in a hotel room that has a mini kitchen or fridge, you can prepare your food ahead of time. Make enough puree to cover the duration of your stay, place it in Sage Spoonfuls jars, and pack it in your cooler, with the frozen ice pack. When you get to your destination put the food in the refrigerator or freezer. You can then serve it as you would at home.

Keep in mind that you can always heat your baby's meals in your bottle warmer. Of course, don't forget extra bibs and spoons. Pack some empty Sage Spoonfuls jars to serve the food in—they're easy to travel with because they stack, won't break, and are dishwasher safe.

Your cooler holds 12 Sage Spoonfuls jars and each jar holds up to 4 ounces of food. This means that you can travel with as much as 48 ounces of food for your baby!

* If your baby is eating 4 oz of solid food per day, you will have enough food to last 12 days.
* If he is eating 6 oz of solid food per day, you will have enough food for 8 days.
* If she is eating 8 oz of solid food per day, you will have enough food for 6 days.
* If he is eating 12 oz of solid food per day, you will have enough food for 4 days.

If there is no kitchen or fridge at your destination

If no kitchen or refrigerator will be available to you at your destination, stick with no-cook purees. Bananas and avocados can be mashed with a spoon or fork and served in Sage Spoonfuls jars. You can even pack your food processor to prepare other no-cook purees, like pear, plum, fresh berries, other ripe fruits, and pre-cooked beans.

These no-cook foods can be mixed with breast milk or formula and a baby cereal, placed in a Sage Spoonfuls jar, and warmed in your bottle warmer. You can also buy yogurt or cottage cheese to mix with your no-cook purees for added protein on-the-go. Be sure to pack extra jars, bibs, and spoons.

✳ I do not recommend taking any puree containing meat, poultry, or fish on-the-go. These purees are not suitable for the cooler and should not be out of the refrigerator for more than 1 hour.

RECIPES CHAPTER FIVE

4-6months

I'M READY!

4-6 MONTHS

smooth and creamy

BUTTERNUT SQUASH

CARROT

AVOCADO

APPLE

PARSNIP

PEAR

ZUCCHINI

PEAS

PUMPKIN

BANANA

How will I know my baby is ready to start solids?

According to the American Academy of Pediatrics, babies are usually ready to start on solids between 4–6 months, but every baby is different, so please check with your pediatrician to determine your baby's readiness. Signs that your baby may be ready to begin her culinary journey:

* She can sit up with support
* He can hold his head up and has control of his neck
* She shows interest in and possibly reaches for the food you are eating
* He has doubled his birth weight
* She is still hungry after a bottle feed

While it is important not to start solids too soon—before 4 months; it is equally as important not to start too late. Babies who start solids later than 6 months are more likely to be picky and hesitant in trying new textures.

What are the best first foods for my baby?

The best first foods for your baby are either single grain baby cereals or easy-to-digest, non-allergenic fruits and vegetables. The list of age-appropriate foods in this section is full of delicious choices. Once your baby has tried foods from the list, individually, you can start making yummy combinations. Royce's first food was pureed carrots and Brendan's was a mashed banana.

What texture should the puree be for this stage?

The texture should be very smooth and creamy, with no lumps or anything that would be difficult for your baby to swallow. If you need to thin the puree, add a little cooking water, breast milk, or formula. If you need to thicken it, add a little baby cereal.

When is the best time of day to give my baby a solid meal?

A great time to give your baby a solid meal is in the late morning after her nap. This is a good time because she will be rested, in a good mood, and ready for some yummy puree! Let her drink some of her bottle before offering your puree. That way she will have satisfied a little of her hunger, but won't be completely full yet. Try to feed her in the same place around the same time and start a routine—babies love having a routine. The best place would be in a high chair in the kitchen or dining room.

4–6 MONTHS

How much do I feed my baby at this stage?

At this stage there is no need to worry about how much solid food your baby is eating. Right now, the idea is to get him used to swallowing food from a spoon and excited about mealtime by feeding him a variety of yummy purees.

The first year, your baby's primary source of nutrition is breast milk or formula so be sure to offer a bottle at mealtime (roughly 32 oz of breast milk or formula daily at this stage). However, don't wait for him to finish the entire bottle before offering some puree, because he will be full. Let him take a few sips and then offer the first bite.

For that first meal, start with a teaspoon or two of a single grain baby cereal or a fruit or vegetable from the 4–6 month food list. As your baby gets used to the idea of swallowing food from a spoon, you can introduce new foods and larger portions, before you know it, those teaspoons will turn into tablespoons and then into ounces! In the beginning, it's a good idea to demonstrate how to eat from a spoon so your baby can see what he is supposed to do.

Offer a solid meal once a day for about 2–4 weeks; then, if your baby is ready, you can bump it to 2 solid meals per day. The rest of your baby's feedings will remain the same—either breast milk or formula. The size of the solid meal will depend on your baby. He may only take a few bites or he may devour the whole thing and want more.

Keep in mind that it's not about "cleaning your plate"; it's about enjoying the new experience of eating food. Follow your baby's cues. He is finished when he turns his head away, starts spitting the food out, or swats at the spoon. Just like us, sometimes babies are really hungry and sometimes they aren't. Never try to force feed—mealtime is supposed to be an enjoyable experience. However, if your baby shows signs of a serious decrease in appetite, consult his pediatrician.

I've heard that giving your baby a fruit first will give him a sweet tooth, and he won't like vegetables.

It has been my experience that it really doesn't matter if you introduce a fruit first or a vegetable first. Babies will eat what tastes good to them. Royce had carrots first and Brendan had a banana first. They both like fruits and vegetables equally. I recommend alternating between fruits and vegetables. For example, if you gave your baby peas as his first food, try apples next. Or if his first taste was banana, try offering zucchini next.

FREQUENTLY ASKED QUESTIONS

 What if my baby doesn't swallow the food or doesn't seem to like it?

Don't stress if your baby spits the food out in the beginning—in fact, it is a natural reflex. Some babies take to swallowing solid food right away and others take a few days or even weeks to get the hang of it. If your baby is consistently thrusting his tongue out when you try to feed him, wait a few days or a week and then try again. I started both of my boys on solids at 5 months; Royce took a week to get used to the idea of swallowing food, but Brendan took to it on the first bite, and he was a preemie!

It's important to have patience and follow your baby's cues. Never force feed—the point is to teach your child the joys of eating and that mealtime is really fun!

 I'm feeling a little anxious about starting my baby on solids. What if I do something wrong?

It's only natural to be a little anxious or nervous about starting solids, but try not to worry—this is an exciting time for both you and your baby. If you follow the guidelines in this book and the advice of your pediatrician, you can't go wrong!

 How much time should I set aside for a solid meal?

Starting your baby on solids is an exciting journey; be sure to allocate enough time for his feedings. A meal could take 5 minutes or 15 minutes—it's up to your baby. It you don't leave enough time for the meal it could really backfire and make a stressful situation out of something that should be enjoyable. If you are stressed or in a hurry, he will sense it and start attaching negative feelings towards mealtime.

I also recommend taking distractions away, from both you and your baby, during mealtime. Whenever possible, turn off the TV and put down the cell phone. Mealtime is a fantastic time to bond with your baby. I love to play relaxing music during mealtime, especially at dinner.

banana

1 Large Banana = 4 oz puree

* Peel the banana, break it in half and place in a bowl.
* Mash with the back of a fork or spoon until smooth and serve. Add breast milk or formula, if needed, to thin puree.
* Banana puree can be stored in your Sage Spoonfuls jars for 1 day in the refrigerator and up to 3 months in the freezer. Some discoloration during storage can be expected.
* **No-cook puree!**

Serving
Banana puree tastes great at room temperature, warm, or cool. For a creamier consistency with added nutrition, mix puree with a little breast milk or formula and a baby cereal (rice or oatmeal) and serve warm. For extra flavor, add a pinch of cinnamon.

On-The-Go
Stored in Sage Spoonfuls jars, banana puree will stay fresh in your cooler, with the frozen ice pack, for up to 12 hours and out of the refrigerator or cooler for up to 2 hours. Banana puree can also be easily prepared while on-the-go; pack a whole banana, a spoon, and an empty Sage Spoonfuls jar. When it's time to eat, mash the banana in the jar and serve.

All About Banana
Banana puree is one of the best first foods for your baby. It is full of nutrients, is easy to digest, and is non-allergenic. Bananas are binding and can be helpful when your baby has diarrhea. They are also a comfort food and can be soothing when your baby isn't feeling well. Look for bananas that have a nice yellow color and some brown speckles. Under ripe or green bananas do not have the same flavor or creamy consistency as ripe bananas. Allow them to ripen on your counter. Ripe bananas will stay fresh at room temperature for 3–5 days.

4–6 MONTHS AND UP

EXCELLENT SOURCE OF:
VITAMIN B6
VITAMIN C
MANGANESE
FIBER
POTASSIUM

GOOD SOURCE OF:
CARBOHYDRATES
MAGNESIUM
FOLATE
RIBOFLAVIN
COPPER
PANTOTHENIC ACID
NIACIN

ALSO CONTAINS:
PROTEIN
THIAMIN
PHOSPHORUS
VITAMIN A
IRON
SELENIUM
ZINC
CALCIUM
VITAMIN E
VITAMIN K

SUITABLE FOR
REFRIGERATOR
OR FREEZER

Yummy Combinations With Banana

With Fruit

Banana and Apple
Banana and Pear
Banana and Avocado

Combine purees in equal parts. They taste great warm and cool. Banana with avocado can also be served at room temperature. Try mixing yummy combo with a little breast milk or formula and a baby cereal (rice or oatmeal) and serve warm. With the exception of avocado, add a pinch of cinnamon for extra flavor. These combinations will stay fresh in your cooler, with the frozen ice pack, for 12 hours and out of the refrigerator or cooler for 2 hours. Banana and avocado is best when mashed fresh just before serving.

With Vegetables

Banana and Sweet Potato
Banana and Pumpkin
Banana and Butternut Squash
Banana and Parsnip

Banana, Apple, and Parsnip
Banana, Apple, and Pumpkin
Banana, Apple, and Butternut Squash
Banana, Pear, and Parsnip

Combine purees in equal parts. They taste great warm and cool. Try mixing yummy combo with a little breast milk or formula and a baby cereal (rice, millet, or barley) and serve warm. For extra flavor, add a pinch of cinnamon. These combos will stay fresh in your cooler, with the frozen ice pack, for 12 hours or out of the refrigerator or cooler for 2 hours. Some discoloration of the banana can be expected.

4–6 MONTHS

pear

1 Medium Pear = 4 oz puree

GOOD SOURCE OF:
FIBER
VITAMIN C
VITAMIN K

ALSO CONTAINS:
CARBOHYDRATES
COPPER
POTASSIUM
MANGANESE
MAGNESIUM
FOLATE
RIBOFLAVIN
VITAMIN B6
VITAMIN E
VITAMIN A
THIAMIN
NIACIN
PANTOTHENIC ACID
CALCIUM
IRON
ZINC
PROTEIN

SUITABLE FOR
REFRIGERATOR
AND FREEZER

* Wash pear thoroughly under cold running water, peel, core, and chop.
* Place pear in steamer basket and steam for about 3–5 minutes until tender.
* Puree until smooth, using an immersion blender or food processor
  Pears are naturally juicy so you won't need additional liquid for thinning.
* Let cool and serve or store.
* Pear puree can be stored in Sage Spoonfuls jars for up to 3 days in the refrigerator or up to 3 months in the freezer. Some slight discoloration during storage can be expected.

Serving
Pear puree tastes great both warm and cool. For a creamier consistency with added nutrition, mix puree with a little breast milk or formula and a baby cereal (rice or oatmeal) and serve warm. For extra flavor, add a pinch of cinnamon.

On-The-Go
Stored in Sage Spoonfuls jars, pear puree will stay fresh in your cooler, with the frozen ice pack, for up to 12 hours and out of the refrigerator or cooler for up to 2 hours.

All About Pear
Pear puree makes a great first food—it has a naturally sweet flavor and soft texture that babies love. It is easy to digest and is non-allergenic. Pear puree is high in fiber and can be helpful when your baby is constipated. It can also help if your baby suffers from acid reflux. Semi-frozen pear puree is a delicious way to sooth a teething baby's sore gums. Pears come in many varieties—Bartlett and Anjou are my favorites. Look for pears that are slightly soft when squeezed. Let under ripe pears ripen on your counter. Whole ripe pears will stay fresh at room temperature or in the refrigerator for 3–5 days.

Yummy Combinations With Pear

With Fruit

Pear and Apple
Pear and Banana

Combine purees in equal parts. They taste great both warm and cool. Try mixing yummy combo with a little breast milk or formula and a baby cereal (rice or oatmeal) and serve warm. For extra flavor, add a pinch of cinnamon. These combinations will stay fresh in your cooler, with the frozen ice pack, for 12 hours and out of the refrigerator or cooler for 2 hours.

With Vegetables

Pear and Butternut Squash
Pear and Pea
Pear and Parsnip
Pear and Pumpkin
Pear and Potato

Pear and Sweet Potato
Pear, Parsnip, and Butternut Squash
Pear, Banana, and Pumpkin
Pear, Apple, and Butternut Squash
Pear, Banana, and Sweet Potato

Combine purees in equal parts. They taste great warm and cool. Try mixing yummy combo with a little breast milk or formula and a baby cereal (rice, millet, or barley) and serve warm. With the exception of peas and potato, add a pinch of cinnamon for extra flavor. These combinations will stay fresh in your cooler, with the frozen ice pack, for 12 hours and out of the refrigerator or cooler for 2 hours.

apple

3 Medium Apples = 10 oz puree

GOOD SOURCE OF:
VITAMIN C
FIBER

ALSO CONTAINS:
CARBOHYDRATES
POTASSIUM
RIBOFLAVIN
VITAMIN B6
COPPER
MANGANESE
VITAMIN A
VITAMIN K
THIAMIN
PANTOTHENIC ACID
CALCIUM
PHOSPHORUS
MAGNESIUM

SUITABLE FOR
REFRIGERATOR
AND FREEZER

✳ Wash apples thoroughly under cold running water, peel, core, and chop.

✳ Place apples in steamer basket and steam for 5–7 minutes, until tender.

✳ Puree until smooth using an immersion blender or food processor. Add cooking water, breast milk, or formula, if needed, to thin puree.

✳ Let cool and serve or store.

✳ Apple puree can be stored in Sage Spoonfuls jars for up to 3 days in the refrigerator or up to 3 months in the freezer.

Serving
Apple puree tastes great both warm and cool. For a creamier consistency with added nutrition, mix puree with a little breast milk or formula and baby cereal (rice or oatmeal) and serve warm. For extra flavor, add a pinch of cinnamon.

On-The-Go
Stored in Sage Spoonfuls jars, apple puree will stay fresh in your cooler, with the frozen ice pack, for up to 12 hours and out of the refrigerator or cooler for up to 2 hours.

All About Apple
Apple puree is a perfect first food for your baby, it tastes great, is easy to digest and is not allergenic. Most varieties of apple, such as Delicious (Red and Golden), Fuji, Honeycrisp, and Gala, make yummy puree. Avoid tart varieties like Granny Smith or Pippin. Red Delicious and Gala both rank on the USDA's top 20 list of antioxidant rich foods. Apple puree can be helpful when your baby is constipated or has diarrhea. Semi-frozen apple puree is very soothing on a teething baby's sore gums. Look for apples that are firm to the touch and are bruise-free. Whole apples can be stored at room temperature or in the refrigerator for up to 2 weeks.

Yummy Combinations With Apple

With Fruit

*

Apple and Banana
Apple and Pear

Combine purees in equal parts. They taste great both warm and cool. Try mixing yummy combo with a little breast milk or formula and a baby cereal (rice or oatmeal) and serve warm. For extra flavor, add a pinch of cinnamon. These combinations will stay fresh in your cooler, with the frozen ice pack, for 12 hours and out of the refrigerator or cooler for 2 hours. Some discoloration in the banana mixture may occur.

With Vegetables

*

Apple and Sweet Potato
Apple and Butternut Squash
Apple and Pumpkin
Apple and Parsnip
Apple and Carrot
Apple and Zucchini

Apple, Zucchini, and Carrot
Apple, Carrot, and Parsnip
Apple, Sweet Potato, and Pumpkin
Apple, Pumpkin, and Parsnip
Apple, Carrot, and Butternut Squash
Apple, Butternut Squash, and Pear

Combine purees in equal parts. They taste great warm and cool. Try mixing yummy combo with a little breast milk or formula and a baby cereal (rice, barley, or millet) and serve warm. With the exception of zucchini, add a pinch of cinnamon for extra flavor. These combinations will stay fresh in your cooler, with the frozen ice pack, for 12 hours and out of the refrigerator or cooler for 2 hours.

avocado

½ Avocado = 2 oz puree

* Cut a ripe avocado in half lengthwise around the pit and twist to open.
* Scoop out the flesh with a spoon and place in a bowl.
* Puree until smooth, using the back of a fork, and serve. Add breast milk or formula to thin puree, if needed.
* Place the half with the pit in an airtight bag. It will stay fresh in the refrigerator for 1 day; slight discoloration can be expected. When you want to serve the second half, remove and discard the pit before preparing.
* **No-cook puree!**

EXCELLENT SOURCE OF:
FIBER
VITAMIN K
FOLATE
VITAMIN C
PANTOTHENIC ACID
POTASSIUM

GOOD SOURCE OF:
VITAMIN B6
VITAMIN E
COPPER
NIACIN
RIBOFLAVIN
MAGNESIUM
MANGANESE
PHOSPHORUS
THIAMIN
ZINC
PROTEIN
IRON

ALSO CONTAINS:
CARBOHYDRATES
VITAMIN A
CALCIUM
SELENIUM

NOT SUITABLE
FOR REFRIGERATOR
AND FREEZER

Serving
Avocado puree tastes great at room temperature, warm or cool. It is best served shortly after preparing.

On-The-Go
Avocado puree is not suitable for on-the-go because it discolors and oxidizes shortly after preparation, which affects its taste. However, whole avocados travel very well and are a no-cook puree; they can be prepared once at your destination. Bring along extra Sage Spoonfuls jars to serve in.

All About Avocado
Avocados are one of nature's superfoods. They have nearly 3 times the amount of potassium as bananas and are high in the antioxidant lutein, which helps promote healthy skin and eyes. Avocados are also a great source of mono-unsaturated fat, which helps develop the central nervous system and brain. Look for avocados with an even green color and that give a little when squeezed. Avoid ones that are over ripe or are very soft. Let under ripe avocados ripen on your counter. Ripe avocados will stay fresh at room temperature for up to 3 days or up to 7 days, when stored in the refrigerator.

Yummy Combinations With Avocado

With Fruit

Avocado and Banana

*

Combine purees in equal parts. This combo tastes great at room temperature, warm or cool. Try mixing yummy combo with a little breast milk or formula and a baby cereal (rice or oatmeal) and serve warm. Serve shortly after preparing to avoid discoloration. This combo is not suitable for on-the-go. However, it is easy to make fresh once at your destination, because both foods are no-cook.

With Vegetables

Avocado and Butternut Squash
Avocado and Pumpkin
Avocado and Sweet Potato

*

Combine purees in equal parts. These combos taste great warm or cool. Try mixing yummy combo with a little breast milk or formula and a baby cereal (rice, barley, or millet) and serve warm. Butternut squash, pumpkin, and sweet potato purees will stay fresh in your cooler, with the frozen ice pack, for 12 hours and out of the refrigerator or cooler for 2 hours. Mash the avocado into the purees just before serving to avoid discoloration.

butternut squash

1 Large Butternut Squash = 25 oz puree

4-6 MONTHS AND UP

EXCELLENT SOURCE OF:
VITAMIN A
VITAMIN C

GOOD SOURCE OF:
POTASSIUM
MANGANESE
MAGNESIUM
VITAMIN B6
FIBER
VITAMIN E
FOLATE
THIAMIN
NIACIN
CALCIUM
PANTOTHENIC ACID

ALSO CONTAINS:
IRON
PHOSPHORUS
COPPER
PROTEIN
VITAMIN K
RIBOFLAVIN
ZINC
SELENIUM

SUITABLE FOR
REFRIGERATOR
AND FREEZER

* Preheat oven to 450 degrees and line a baking sheet with unbleached parchment paper.
* Cut the butternut squash in half lengthwise, scoop out the seeds and stringy fibers with a spoon and discard.
* Place squash cut side down on the baking sheet and place in oven on the middle rack.
* Roast for about 45 minutes, until squash is easily pierced with a fork.
* Let cool for 5 minutes then scoop the squash out of the skin with a spoon or just peel the skin right off. It's best to use an oven mitt when handling the roasted squash so you don't burn your hand.
* Puree until smooth, using an immersion blender or food processor. Butternut squash is naturally juicy, so you won't need additional liquid for thinning.
* Let cool and serve or store.
* Butternut squash puree can be stored in Sage Spoonfuls jars for up to 3 days in the refrigerator and up to 3 months in the freezer.

Serving
Butternut Squash puree tastes great both warm and cool. For a creamier consistency with added nutrition, mix puree with a little breast milk or formula and a baby cereal (rice, oatmeal, millet, or barley) and serve warm. For extra flavor, add a pinch of cinnamon.

On-The-Go
Stored in Sage Spoonfuls jars, butternut squash puree will stay fresh in your cooler, with the frozen ice pack, for up to 12 hours and out of the refrigerator or cooler for up to 2 hours.

All About Butternut Squash
Butternut squash puree is a wonderful first food for your baby. It has a mild sweet taste, is easy to digest, and is not allergenic. Butternut squash are full of nutrients, especially disease-fighting carotenes. This puree can be soothing when your baby has an upset stomach. Look for butternut squash that are firm to the touch and heavy for their size. Whole butternut squash are hearty and have a long shelf life. They will stay fresh at room temperature for about one month.

Yummy Combinations With Butternut Squash

With Fruit

Butternut Squash and Banana
Butternut Squash and Apple
Butternut Squash and Pear

Butternut Squash, Banana, and Apple
Butternut Squash, Banana, and Pear
Butternut Squash, Pear, and Apple

Combine purees in equal parts. They taste great warm or cool. Try mixing yummy combo with a little breast milk or formula and a baby cereal (rice or oatmeal) and serve warm. Add a pinch of cinnamon for extra flavor. These combos will stay fresh in your cooler, with the frozen ice pack, for 12 hours and out of the refrigerator or cooler for 2 hours.

With Vegetables

Butternut Squash and Pea
Butternut Squash and Parsnip
Butternut Squash and Potato
Butternut Squash and Pumpkin
Butternut Squash and Carrot
Butternut Squash and Sweet Potato
Butternut Squash, Parsnip, and Apple

Butternut Squash, Potato, and Apple
Butternut Squash, Pumpkin, and Apple
Butternut Squash, Pumpkin, and Pea
Butternut Squash, Pea, and Carrot
Butternut Squash, Carrot, and Apple
Butternut Squash, Pumpkin, and Banana
Butternut Squash, Parsnip, and Pear

Combine purees in equal parts. They taste great warm or cool. Try mixing yummy combo with a little breast milk or formula and a baby cereal (rice, millet, or barley) and serve warm. Add a pinch of cinnamon for extra flavor. These combos will stay fresh in your cooler, with the frozen ice pack, for 12 hours or out of the refrigerator or cooler for 2 hours.

4–6 MONTHS

peas

2 Cups Frozen Peas = 8 oz puree

EXCELLENT SOURCE OF:
VITAMIN C
VITAMIN K
FIBER
MANGANESE
THIAMIN
FOLATE
VITAMIN A

GOOD SOURCE OF:
PHOSPHORUS
PROTEIN
NIACIN
COPPER
MAGNESIUM
ZINC
VITAMIN B6
IRON
RIBOFLAVIN
POTASSIUM

ALSO CONTAINS:
CARBOHYDRATES
SELENIUM
CALCIUM
PANTOTHENIC ACID
VITAMIN E

SUITABLE FOR
REFRIGERATOR
AND FREEZER

* Place peas in steamer basket and steam for 7–9 minutes, until bright green and tender. If using fresh peas, de-shell and wash thoroughly before steaming.

* Puree until smooth using a food processor. Add cooking water, breast milk or formula, as needed, to thin puree.

* Let cool and serve or store.

* Pea puree can be stored in Sage Spoonfuls jars for up to 3 days in refrigerator or up to 3 months in freezer. It will thicken during storage; add a little purified water, breast milk, or formula to thin when reheating.

Serving
Pea puree tastes great both warm and cool. For a creamier consistency with added nutrition, mix puree with a little breast milk or formula and a baby cereal (rice, barley, or millet) and serve warm. For extra flavor, add a touch of fresh mint while pureeing.

On-The-Go
Stored in Sage Spoonfuls jars, pea puree will stay fresh in your cooler, with the frozen ice pack, for up to 12 hours and out of the refrigerator or cooler for up to 2 hours.

All About Peas
Pea puree makes a great first food for your baby. It has a delicious sweet taste that babies love, is easy to digest, and is not allergenic. Peas are packed with nutrients and antioxidants. I like using frozen peas, because they are just as nutritious as fresh peas, but without the hassle of having to de-shell. If you are using fresh peas, look for pea pods that are bright green and firm. Unshelled fresh peas will stay fresh in your refrigerator for about a week.

Yummy Combinations With Peas

With Fruit

*

Pea and Pear
Pea and Apple

Combine purees in equal parts. They taste great both warm and cool. Try mixing yummy combo with a little breast milk or formula and a baby cereal (rice or oatmeal) and serve warm. These combos will stay fresh in your cooler, with the frozen ice pack, for 12 hours and out of the refrigerator or cooler for 2 hours.

With Vegetable

*

Pea and Potato
Pea and Carrot
Pea and Parsnip
Pea and Pumpkin
Pea and Sweet Potato
Pea and Butternut Squash

Pea, Parsnip, and Potato
Pea, Carrot, and Potato
Pea, Sweet Potato, and Carrot
Pea, Carrot, and Pumpkin
Pea, Zucchini, and Potato
Pea, Butternut Squash, and Carrot

Combine purees in equal parts. They taste best warm, but can also be served cool. Try mixing yummy combo with a little breast milk or formula and a baby cereal (rice, barley, or millet) and serve warm. These combos will stay fresh in your cooler, with the frozen ice pack, for 12 hours and out of the refrigerator or cooler for 2 hours.

4–6 MONTHS

EXCELLENT SOURCE OF:
VITAMIN A

GOOD SOURCE OF:
VITAMIN K
FIBER
VITAMIN C
POTASSIUM
MANGANESE
VITAMIN B6
THIAMIN
NIACIN
FOLATE

ALSO CONTAINS:
VITAMIN E
RIBOFLAVIN
CARBOHYDRATES
CALCIUM
MAGNESIUM
PHOSPHORUS
SODIUM
PANTOTHENIC ACID
COPPER
ZINC
IRON
PROTEIN

SUITABLE FOR
REFRIGERATOR
AND FREEZER

carrot

5 Medium Carrots = 12 oz puree

* Wash carrots thoroughly under cold running water, cut off and discard the green stems, peel and chop.
* Place carrots in steamer basket and steam for 7–9 minutes until tender.
* Puree until smooth using an immersion blender or food processor. Add purified water, breast milk, or formula, as needed, to thin puree. Due to higher nitrate levels in carrots, do not thin puree with the cooking water.
* Let cool and serve or store.
* Carrot puree can be stored in Sage Spoonfuls jars for up to 3 days in the refrigerator or up to 3 months in the freezer.

Serving
Carrot puree tastes great both warm and cool. For a creamier consistency with added nutrition, mix puree with a little breast milk or formula and a baby cereal (rice, barley, or millet) and serve warm. Add a pinch of cinnamon or ginger for extra flavor.

On-The-Go
Stored in Sage Spoonfuls jars, carrot puree will stay fresh in your cooler, with the frozen ice pack, for up to 12 hours and out of the refrigerator or cooler for up to 2 hours.

All About Carrot
Carrot puree makes a good first food for your baby. It has a mild taste and is high in nutrients and disease-fighting antioxidants. It is also easy to digest and is not allergenic. Carrots are incredibly rich in Vitamin A, making them great for your baby's eyesight. Whenever possible, buy organic carrots—they are lower in nitrates than conventionally grown. Look for carrots that are crack-free, have a nice orange color, and are firm, not rubbery. Whole carrots will stay fresh in a plastic bag in the refrigerator for 10–14 days.

Yummy Combinations With Carrot

With Fruit

*

Carrot and Apple
Carrot and Pear

Combine purees in equal parts. They taste great both warm and cool. Try mixing yummy combo with a little breast milk or formula and a baby cereal (rice or oatmeal) and serve warm. Add a pinch of cinnamon for extra flavor. These combos will stay fresh in your cooler, with the frozen ice pack, for 12 hours and out of the refrigerator or cooler for 2 hours.

With Vegetables

*

Carrot and Butternut Squash
Carrot and Potato
Carrot and Pea
Carrot and Zucchini
Carrot and Parsnip
Carrot and Sweet Potato

Carrot, Potato, and Pea
Carrot, Potato, and Zucchini
Carrot, Parsnip, and Apple
Carrot, Potato, and Parsnip
Carrot, Butternut Squash, and Apple
Carrot, Sweet Potato, and Parsnip

Combine purees in equal parts. They taste great warm and cool. Try mixing yummy combo with a little breast milk or formula and a baby cereal (rice, barley, or millet) and serve warm. These combos will stay fresh in your cooler, with the frozen ice pack, for 12 hours and out of the refrigerator or cooler for 2 hours.

zucchini

4 Medium Zucchini = 10 oz puree

4–6 MONTHS AND UP

EXCELLENT SOURCE OF:
VITAMIN C

GOOD SOURCE OF:
VITAMIN B6
MANGANESE
RIBOFLAVIN
FOLATE
POTASSIUM
VITAMIN K

ALSO CONTAINS:
MAGNESIUM
PHOSPHORUS
FIBER
VITAMIN A
THIAMIN
PROTEIN
NIACIN
COPPER
PANTOTHENIC ACID
CALCIUM
IRON
ZINC
SODIUM
VITAMIN E

SUITABLE FOR
REFRIGERATOR
AND FREEZER

* Wash zucchini thoroughly under cold running water, peel and chop. If the zucchini are organic, you don't need to peel.

* Place zucchini in steamer basket and steam for 5–7 minutes, until tender.

* Puree until smooth using an immersion blender or food processor. Zucchini are naturally watery, so you won't need additional liquid to thin puree.

* Let cool and serve or store.

* Zucchini puree can be stored in your Sage Spoonfuls jars for up to 3 days in the refrigerator or up to 3 months in the freezer.

Serving
Zucchini puree tastes great both warm and cool. For a creamier consistency with added nutrition, mix puree with a little breast milk or formula and a baby cereal (rice, barley, or millet) and serve warm.

On-The-Go
Stored in Sage Spoonfuls jars, zucchini puree will stay fresh in your cooler, with the frozen ice pack, for up to 12 hours and out of the refrigerator or cooler for up to 2 hours.

All About Zucchini
Zucchini puree makes a great first food, because it has a mild taste, is easily digested, and is not allergenic. Zucchini have very tender, edible seeds and skin, which contain most of the nutrients. Try to buy organic whenever possible so your baby can eat the nutrient-rich skin. Look for zucchini that are medium sized, have an even green color, and are blemish-free. Whole zucchini can be stored in a plastic bag in your refrigerator for up to a week.

Yummy Combinations With Zucchini

With Fruit

*

Zucchini and Apple
Zucchini and Pear

Combine purees in equal parts. They taste great both warm and cool. Try mixing yummy combo with a little breast milk or formula and a baby cereal (rice, barley, or millet) and serve warm. These combos will stay fresh in your cooler, with the frozen ice pack, for 12 hours and out of the refrigerator or cooler for 2 hours.

With Vegetables

*

Zucchini and Potato
Zucchini and Carrot
Zucchini and Parsnip
Zucchini, Potato, and Pea
Zucchini, Potato, and Carrot

Combine purees in equal parts. They taste best warm, but can also be served cool. Try mixing yummy combo with a little breast milk or formula and a baby cereal (rice, barley, or millet) and serve warm. These combos will stay fresh in your cooler, with the frozen ice pack, for 12 hours and out of the refrigerator or cooler for 2 hours.

sweet potato

1 Medium Sweet Potato = 10 oz puree

EXCELLENT SOURCE OF:
VITAMIN A

GOOD SOURCE OF:
MANGANESE
FIBER
VITAMIN B6
POTASSIUM
PANTOTHENIC ACID
COPPER
CARBOHYDRATES
MAGNESIUM
THIAMIN
PHOSPHORUS

ALSO CONTAINS:
VITAMIN C
RIBOFLAVIN
IRON
NIACIN
FOLATE
CALCIUM
PROTEIN
VITAMIN K
SODIUM
ZINC
VITAMIN E
SELENIUM

SUITABLE FOR
REFRIGERATOR
AND FREEZER

✳ Wash sweet potato thoroughly under cold running water, peel and chop.

✳ Place sweet potato in steamer basket and steam for about 15 minutes, until tender.

✳ Puree until smooth by mashing with the back of a fork or working through a food mill.

✳ Add cooking water, breast milk, or formula, as needed, to thin puree to a creamy consistency. Do not puree sweet potato with a blender or food processor. The texture will become too thick and starchy.

✳ Let cool and serve or store.

✳ Sweet potato puree can be stored in Sage Spoonfuls jars for up to 3 days, in the refrigerator, and up to 3 months in the freezer. It will thicken during storage; add a little breast milk, formula or purified water to thin puree when reheating.

✳ To roast: cut sweet potato in half lengthwise, place cut side down on a baking sheet lined with parchment paper, roast at 425 degrees for 35–45 minutes, scoop out flesh with a spoon and puree.

Serving
Sweet potato puree tastes great both warm and cool. For a creamier consistency with added nutrition, mix puree with a little breast milk or formula and a baby cereal (rice, barley, or millet) and serve warm. For extra flavor, add a pinch of cinnamon.

On-The-Go
Stored in Sage Spoonfuls jars, sweet potato puree will stay fresh in your cooler, with the frozen ice pack, for up to 12 hours or out of the refrigerator or cooler for up to 2 hours.

All About Sweet Potato
Sweet potatoes are nutritional powerhouses. They are full of disease-fighting carotenes and antioxidants. Sweet potato puree has a creamy, sweet flavor and makes a great staple in your baby's diet. There are many varieties of sweet potato. All make delicious puree. Asian sweet potatoes have white flesh while yams have a deep orange flesh. Look for sweet potatoes that are firm to the touch and show no signs of sprouting or discoloration. Whole sweet potatoes can be stored at room temperature for up to 10 days.

Yummy Combinations With Sweet Potato

With Fruit

Sweet Potato and Apple
Sweet Potato and Banana

Sweet Potato and Pear
Sweet Potato, Banana, and Apple

Combine purees in equal parts. They taste great both warm and cool.
Try mixing yummy combo with a little breast milk or formula and a baby
cereal (rice or oatmeal) and serve warm. For extra flavor, add a pinch
of cinnamon. These combos will stay fresh in your cooler, with the frozen
ice pack, for 12 hours and out of the refrigerator or cooler for 2 hours.

**With
Vegetables**

Sweet Potato and Parsnip
Sweet Potato and Pea
Sweet Potato and Pumpkin
Sweet Potato and Carrot
Sweet Potato, Carrot, and Pea

Sweet Potato, Pumpkin, and Apple
Sweet Potato, Carrot, and Parsnip
Sweet Potato, Parsnip, and Apple
Sweet Potato, Pumpkin, and Banana
Sweet Potato and Butternut Squash

Combine purees in equal parts. They taste best warm, but can also
be served cool. Try mixing yummy combo with a little breast milk or
formula and a baby cereal (rice, millet, or barley). With the exception
of peas, add a pinch of cinnamon for extra flavor. These combos will
stay fresh in your cooler, with the frozen ice pack, for 12 hours and out
of the refrigerator or cooler for 2 hours.

parsnip

4 Medium Parsnips = 10 oz puree

4-6 MONTHS AND UP

* Wash parsnips thoroughly under cold running water, peel and chop.
* Place in steamer basket and steam for 8–10 minutes until tender.
* Puree until smooth using an immersion blender or food processor. Add purified water, breast milk, or formula, as needed, to thin puree.
* Let cool and serve or store.
* Parsnip puree can be stored in Sage Spoonfuls jars for up to 3 months in refrigerator and up to 3 months in freezer.

EXCELLENT SOURCE OF:
VITAMIN C
VITAMIN K
MANGANESE
FIBER
FOLATE

GOOD SOURCE OF:
POTASSIUM
MAGNESIUM
VITAMIN E
PHOSPHORUS
THIAMIN
PANTOTHENIC ACID
COPPER
CARBOHYDRATES

ALSO CONTAINS:
VITAMIN B6
NIACIN
CALCIUM
ZINC
RIBOFLAVIN
IRON
PROTEIN
SELENIUM
SODIUM

SUITABLE FOR
REFRIGERATOR
AND FREEZER

Serving
Parsnip puree tastes best warm, but can also be served cool. For a creamier consistency with added nutrition, mix puree with a little breast milk or formula and a baby cereal (rice, barley, or millet) and serve warm. For extra flavor, add a pinch of cinnamon.

On-The-Go
Stored in Sage Spoonfuls jars, parsnip puree will stay fresh in your cooler, with the frozen ice pack, for up to 12 hours and out of the refrigerator or cooler for up to 2 hours.

All About Parsnip
Parsnip puree makes a delicious food for your baby. It is easy to digest, is non allergenic, and tastes great. Parsnip puree has a hearty, earthy, yet sweet taste and aroma that babies love. It is not only delicious on its own but is a nutritious base to mix with other foods. Parsnips look like big white carrots, but have the consistency of potatoes. Choose parsnips that are firm and not rubbery. Whole parsnips will stay fresh in a plastic bag in the refrigerator for up to 2 weeks.

Yummy Combinations With Parsnip

With Fruit

*

Parsnip and Apple
Parsnip and Pear

Parsnip and Banana

Combine purees in equal parts. These combinations taste great both warm and cool. Try mixing yummy combo with a little breast milk or formula and a baby cereal (rice or oatmeal) and serve warm. For extra flavor, add a pinch of cinnamon. These combinations will stay fresh in your cooler, with the frozen ice pack, for 12 hours and out of the refrigerator or cooler for 2 hours.

**With
Vegetables**

*

Parsnip and Pea
Parsnip and Zucchini
Parsnip and Carrot
Parsnip and Pumpkin
Parsnip and Potato
Parsnip and Butternut Squash

Parsnip and Sweet Potato
Parsnip, Carrot, and Apple
Parsnip, Carrot, and Sweet Potato
Parsnip, Butternut Squash, and Apple
Parsnip, Pumpkin, and Butternut Squash
Parsnip, Sweet Potato, and Banana

Combine purees in equal parts. These combinations taste best warm, but can also be served cool. Try mixing yummy combo with a little breast milk or formula and a baby cereal (rice, barley, or millet) and serve warm. With the exception of zucchini and peas, add a pinch of cinnamon for extra flavor. These combinations will stay fresh in your cooler, with the frozen ice pack, for 12 hours and out of the refrigerator or cooler for 2 hours.

pumpkin

1 Medium Baking Pumpkin = 16 oz puree

* Preheat oven to 450 degrees and line a baking sheet with unbleached parchment paper.
* Wash pumpkin thoroughly under cold running water and dry with a paper towel. Cut off stem and discard.
* Slice pumpkin in half lengthwise, scoop out seeds and fibers with a spoon, and discard.
* Place pumpkin cut side down on the baking sheet and place in the oven on the center rack.
* Roast for 35–45 minutes, until easily pierced with a fork. Remove from the oven and let cool for 5–10 minutes.
* Using an oven mitt, pick up the pumpkin, scoop out the flesh with a spoon, and place in a large mixing bowl.
* Puree until smooth, using an immersion blender or food processor. Add purified water, breast milk, or formula, as needed, to thin puree.
* Let cool and serve or store.
* Pumpkin puree can be stored in Sage Spoonfuls jars for up to 3 days in the refrigerator and up to 3 months in the freezer.

Serving
Pumpkin puree tastes great both warm and cool. For a creamier consistency with added nutrition, mix puree with a little breast milk or formula and a baby cereal (rice, millet, or barley) and serve warm. For extra flavor, add a pinch of cinnamon.

On-The-Go
Stored in Sage Spoonfuls jars, pumpkin puree will stay fresh in your cooler, with the frozen ice pack, for up to 12 hours and out of the refrigerator or cooler for up to 2 hours.

All About Pumpkin
Pumpkin puree has a mild sweet taste, is easily digested, and is non allergenic. Pumpkins are rich in disease-fighting carotenes. They also contain lutein, which promotes healthy eyes. Look for smaller baking pumpkins—not the large ones we see at Halloween. Choose pumpkins that are firm to the touch and heavy for their size. Whole pumpkins are very hearty and can be stored at room temperature for up to a month.

Yummy Combinations With Pumpkin

With Fruit

Pumpkin and Pear
Pumpkin and Banana
Pumpkin and Apple

Pumpkin, Banana, and Apple
Pumpkin, Banana, and Pear

Combine purees in equal parts. They taste great warm or cool. Try mixing yummy combo with a little breast milk or formula and a baby cereal (rice or oatmeal) and serve warm. Add a pinch of cinnamon for extra flavor. These combos will stay fresh in your cooler, with the frozen ice pack, for 12 hours and out of the refrigerator or cooler for 2 hours.

With Vegetables

Pumpkin and Pea
Pumpkin and Parsnip
Pumpkin and Potato
Pumpkin and Sweet Potato
Pumpkin and Butternut Squash

Pumpkin, Parsnip, and Pear
Pumpkin, Parsnip, and Apple
Pumpkin, Banana, and Butternut Squash
Pumpkin, Banana, and Sweet Potato
Pumpkin, Apple, and Sweet Potato

Combine purees in equal parts. They taste best warm, but can also be served cool. Try mixing yummy combo with a little breast milk or formula and a baby cereal (rice, millet or barley). With the exception of peas, add a pinch of cinnamon for extra flavor. These combos will stay fresh in your cooler, with the frozen ice pack, for 12 hours and out of the refrigerator or cooler for 2 hours.

potato

1 Medium Potato = 10 oz puree

4–6 MONTHS AND UP

* Wash potato thoroughly under cold running water, peel and chop.
* Place potato into steamer basket and steam for 12–15 minutes, until easily pierced with a fork.
* Puree until smooth by mashing with the back of a fork or working through a food mill. Add cooking water, breast milk, or formula, as needed, to develop a smooth and creamy consistency. Do not puree with a blender or food processor, as the texture will become too starchy.
* Let cool and serve or store.
* Potato puree can be stored in Sage Spoonfuls jars for up to 3 days in the refrigerator or up to 3 months in the freezer. It will thicken during storage; add a little breast milk or formula to thin puree when reheating.

EXCELLENT SOURCE OF:
VITAMIN C
VITAMIN B6
POTASSIUM
FIBER

GOOD SOURCE OF:
MANGANESE
CARBOHYDRATES
MAGNESIUM
PHOSPHORUS
COPPER
THIAMIN
NIACIN
IRON
FOLATE
PROTEIN
PANTOTHENIC ACID
VITAMIN K

ALSO CONTAINS:
RIBOFLAVIN
ZINC
CALCIUM
SELENIUM
SODIUM

Serving
Potato puree tastes best warm. For a creamier consistency with added nutrition, mix puree with a little breast milk or formula and a baby cereal (rice, millet, or barley).

On-The-Go
Stored in Sage Spoonfuls jars, potato puree will stay fresh in your cooler, with the frozen ice pack, for up to 12 hours and out of the refrigerator or cooler for up to 2 hours.

All About Potato
Babies love the creamy taste and texture of potatoes, making them a great base to mix with other foods. There are many different varieties and each one has its own taste. My favorites are the buttery tasting Yukon Gold and the antioxidant-rich Russet. Potato puree can be helpful when your baby has diarrhea or an upset stomach. Look for potatoes that are firm. Avoid ones that are sprouting or discolored, especially with a green tint. Whole potatoes will stay fresh in your cupboard or pantry for about 2 weeks.

SUITABLE FOR
REFRIGERATOR
AND FREEZER

Yummy Combinations With Potato

With Fruit

Potato and Pear
Potato and Apple

Combine purees in equal parts. They taste best warm. Try mixing yummy combo with a little breast milk or formula and a baby cereal (rice, millet, barley, or oatmeal) and serve warm. These combinations will stay fresh in your cooler, with the frozen ice pack, for 12 hours and out of the refrigerator or cooler for 2 hours.

With Vegetables

Potato and Zucchini
Potato and Carrot
Potato and Pea
Potato and Parsnip
Potato and Butternut Squash

Potato, Pea, and Carrot
Potato, Butternut Squash, and Apple
Potato, Parsnip, and Pear
Potato, Zucchini, and Carrot
Potato, Pea, and Pear

Combine purees in equal parts. They taste best warm. Try mixing yummy combo with a little breast milk or formula and a baby cereal (rice, barley, or millet). These combinations will stay fresh in your cooler, with the frozen ice pack, for 12 hours and out of the refrigerator or cooler for 2 hours.

baby rice cereal

¼ Cup Brown Rice = 1 cup Baby Rice Cereal

* Place rice into a standard blender and pulverize until powdery, 1–2 minutes.

* Bring 1½ cups of purified water to a boil in a small saucepan over high heat. Add brown rice powder and let boil for 1 minute.

* Reduce heat to low and cook for 7–10 minutes, stirring frequently with a whisk, until liquid is absorbed. Add purified water, breast milk or formula to thin cereal, if needed.

* Let cool and serve or store.

* Prepared baby rice cereal can be stored in Sage Spoonfuls jars for up to 3 days in the refrigerator or up to 3 months in the freezer. The cereal will thicken during storage; add a little purified water, breast milk, or formula to thin cereal when reheating.

Serving
Baby rice cereal is best served warm. For a creamier consistency with added nutrition, mix cereal with breast milk or formula and a fruit or veggie puree. When your baby is a little older; try mixing baby rice cereal with meat, poultry, fish, and beans.

On-The-Go
Stored in Sage Spoonfuls jars, cooked baby rice cereal will stay fresh in your cooler, with the frozen ice pack, for up to 12 hours and out of the refrigerator or cooler for up to 2 hours.

All About Rice Cereal
Baby rice cereal is a wonderful first food for your baby—it's easy to digest and is non-allergenic. Brown rice is much higher in nutrients than white rice, because it retains its hull. White rice is highly processed, leaving it devoid of many nutrients. While homemade brown rice cereal contains some iron, store bought is usually fortified with extra iron. If you are making your own baby cereal, discuss your baby's iron needs with his pediatrician to be sure he is getting enough. Brown rice cereal makes a great staple in your child's diet. It can be purchased in bulk and, when stored in an airtight container, will stay fresh in the refrigerator for up to 6 months.

4–6 MONTHS AND UP

EXCELLENT SOURCE OF:
MANGANESE
MAGNESIUM
VITAMIN B6
PHOSPHORUS
CARBOHYDRATES

GOOD SOURCE OF:
FIBER
THIAMIN
NIACIN
PROTEIN
PANTOTHENIC ACID
ZINC
COPPER
IRON

ALSO CONTAINS:
POTASSIUM
FOLATE
CALCIUM
RIBOFLAVIN

SUITABLE FOR REFRIGERATOR AND FREEZER

baby oatmeal

½ Cup of Rolled Oats = 1 cup prepared

* Place oats into a standard blender or food processor and pulverize into fine flakes—about 1 minute.

* Bring 1 cup of purified water to a boil in a small saucepan over high heat. Add oat flakes and let boil for 1 minute.

* Reduce heat to low and cook for about 5 minutes, stirring frequently with a whisk, until all the liquid is absorbed. Add purified water, breast milk or formula to thin cereal, if needed.

* Let cool and serve or store.

* Cooked baby oatmeal can be stored in Sage Spoonfuls jars for up to 3 days in the refrigerator or up to 3 months in the freezer. It will thicken during storage; add a little purified water, breast milk, or formula to thin cereal when reheating.

Serving
Oatmeal is best served warm. For a creamier consistency with added nutrition, mix oatmeal with a little breast milk or formula and your baby's favorite fruit puree. For extra flavor, add a pinch of cinnamon.

On-The-Go
Stored in Sage Spoonfuls jars, cooked baby oatmeal will stay fresh in your cooler, with the frozen ice pack, for up to 12 hours and out of the refrigerator or cooler for up to 2 hours.

All About Oatmeal
Oatmeal is a wonderful comfort food with endless flavor combinations—it is a delicious breakfast that your children will enjoy for years to come. Oats are rich in nutrients, including protein and iron. Baby oatmeal makes a great staple in your child's diet. While you can use quicker cooking rolled oats, stay away from oatmeal packets, because they usually have added sugar and preservatives, and the oats lose many of their nutrients during processing. Rolled oats will stay fresh for up to 2 months when stored in an airtight container in a cool, dry place.

4-6 MONTHS AND UP

EXCELLENT SOURCE OF:
MANGANESE
FIBER
PHOSPHORUS
SELENIUM
MAGNESIUM
THIAMIN
PROTEIN
ZINC
CARBOHYDRATES
IRON
COPPER

GOOD SOURCE OF:
PANTOTHENIC ACID
POTASSIUM
RIBOFLAVIN
FOLATE
NIACIN

ALSO CONTAINS:
VITAMIN B6
CALCIUM
VITAMIN E
VITAMIN K

4-6 MONTHS

SUITABLE FOR
REFRIGERATOR
AND FREEZER

baby barley

¼ Cup of Pearl Barley = 1 cup prepared

EXCELLENT SOURCE OF:
FIBER
MANGANESE
SELENIUM
NIACIN

GOOD SOURCE OF:
CARBOHYDRATES
IRON
THIAMIN
ZINC
MAGNESIUM
VITAMIN B6
PHOSPHORUS
COPPER
PROTEIN
RIBOFLAVIN
FOLATE

ALSO CONTAINS:
POTASSIUM
VITAMIN K
PANTOTHENIC ACID
CALCIUM

SUITABLE FOR
REFRIGERATOR
AND FREEZER

* Place barley in a standard blender and pulverize until flakey or powdery—3–5 minutes. Stop the blender halfway through and let the motor rest for a moment, blenders should not run continuously for more than 3 minutes or they could overheat.

* Bring 1 cup of purified water to a boil in a small saucepan over high heat. Add barley flakes and let boil for 1 minute.

* Reduce heat to low and cook for 7–10 minutes, stirring frequently with a whisk, until the water is absorbed. Add purified water, breast milk, or formula to thin cereal, if needed.

* Let cool and serve or store.

* Cooked baby barley cereal can be stored in Sage Spoonfuls jars for up to 3 days in the refrigerator or up to 3 months in the freezer. It will thicken during storage; add purified water, breast milk, or formula to thin cereal when reheating.

Serving
Baby barley cereal is best served warm. For a creamier consistency with added nutrition, mix cereal with a little breast milk or formula and your baby's favorite veggie puree.

On-The-Go
Stored in Sage Spoonfuls jars, cooked baby barley cereal will stay fresh in your cooler, with the frozen ice pack, for up to 12 hours and out of the refrigerator or cooler for up to 2 hours.

All About Barley
Barley makes a good first cereal because it is easy to digest and is non-allergenic. It has a sweet, earthy taste that mixes well with vegetables, and, when your baby is older, meat, poultry, fish and beans. Barley is a good source of iron, which is vital to your baby's red blood cell production. It is also rich in selenium and high in fiber. Barley can be purchased in bulk or prepackaged. When stored in an airtight container, in a cool, dry place, barley will stay fresh for up to 6 months.

baby millet

½ Cup Millet = 1 cup cereal

* Place millet in a standard blender and pulverize into a powder—about 3 minutes.
* Bring 1 ½ cup of purified water to boil in a small saucepan over high heat. Add the millet and let boil for 1 minute.
* Reduce heat to low. Let cook for about 5 minutes, stirring frequently, until all the liquid is absorbed. Add cooking water, breast milk, or formula to thin cereal, if needed.
* Let cool and serve or store.
* Baby millet cereal can be stored in Sage Spoonfuls jars for up to 3 days in the refrigerator or up to 3 months in the freezer. It will thicken during storage; add a little purified water, breast milk or formula to thin cereal when reheating.

Serving
Baby barley cereal is best served warm. For a creamier consistency with added nutrition, mix cereal with a little breast milk or formula and a veggie puree. It is also delicious mixed with meat, poultry, fish, and beans for when your baby is a little older.

On-The-Go
Stored in Sage Spoonfuls jars, cooked baby millet will stay fresh in your cooler, with the frozen ice pack, for up to 12 hours and out of the refrigerator or cooler for up to 2 hours.

All About Millet
Millet is a great first cereal for babies because it is easy to digest and is gluten and wheat-free. While often thought of as a grain, millet is actually a seed. Rich in disease-fighting antioxidants, millet also contains highly absorbable plant-based protein, making it an excellent food for vegetarian babies. Whole grains, such as millet, have been shown to help ward off childhood asthma. Millet can be purchased in bulk or prepackaged. When stored in an airtight container in a cool, dry place, millet will stay fresh for up to 6 months.

4-6 MONTHS AND UP

EXCELLENT SOURCE OF:
MANGANESE
MAGNESIUM
PHOSPHORUS

GOOD SOURCE OF:
CARBOHYDRATES
COPPER
PROTEIN
THIAMIN
NIACIN
ZINC
FIBER
VITAMIN B6
RIBOFLAVIN
FOLATE
IRON
CALCIUM

ALSO CONTAINS:
PANTOTHENIC ACID
POTASSIUM
SELENIUM
VITAMIN K

SUITABLE FOR REFRIGERATOR AND FREEZER

4-6 MONTHS

Notes:

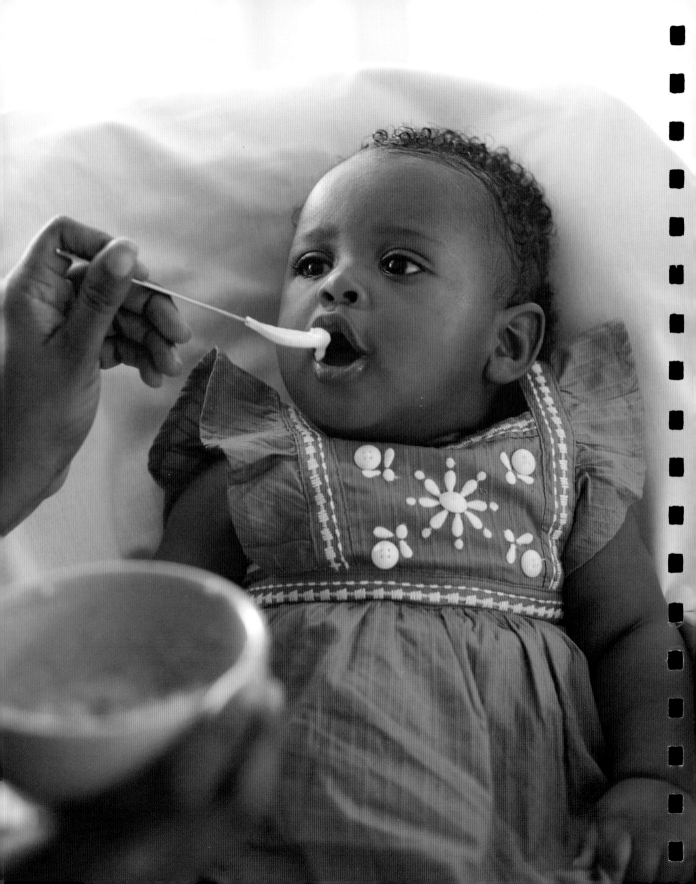

7–9months

THIS IS YUMMY!

7–9 MONTHS

FREQUENTLY ASKED QUESTIONS

 What is the appropriate texture for this age range?

At 4–6 months, the idea was to get your baby used to swallowing solid food. At this stage, the idea is for your baby to learn how to gum food, which is the step before chewing. If your baby is ready, you can start to thicken her purees into a mushy mash. A mushy mash is thicker and lumpier than a smooth and creamy puree. The lumps must be soft so she can gum them. As her teeth come in, continue to play with texture and thickness, but be sure to keep the lumps soft. If they are not soft, your baby could choke.

As far as the texture of baby cereals and grains goes, if your baby is ready, you can now feed him millet without pulverizing it first. Millet is naturally very small in size and cooks up into a perfect mushy mash. The same goes for quinoa and amaranth; they are small in size and cook up nice and mushy. However, if your baby isn't quite ready, please pulverize before cooking or mash/puree before serving. Rice, oatmeal, and barley are larger sized grains and still need to be either pulverized before cooking, or mashed/pureed into smaller pieces before serving.

This is also a good time to introduce small shaped pasta like pastina and stellini, if you feel your baby is ready. These pasta shapes are naturally mushy and the perfect size for this stage.

 Do all foods still need to be cooked?

Your list of no-cook purees just expanded in a big way! Unless otherwise directed by your pediatrician, soft, ripe fruits, like pear and peach, can now be pureed without cooking. This will not only save you time, but it allows your baby to get the most from his food, because the majority of foods lose nutrients when they are cooked. However, vegetables still need to be cooked, and, of course, meat, poultry, and fish need to be cooked all the way through before serving to your baby.

How much solid food should my baby eat at this stage?

During this stage you can move from to 2 to 3 solid meals per day if your baby is ready. Each meal will be between 4–6 ounces. It could be less, it could be more. The size of each meal really depends on your baby, how big her appetite is, and your pediatrician's recommendation. Be sure to keep offering your baby a bottle with her meals (roughly 24–30 ounces of breast milk or formula daily at this stage).

Do I continue introducing new foods one at a time?

Yes, continue introducing new foods one at a time for the first year. As your baby successfully devours each food, your list of yummy combinations will get longer and longer.

Is it okay to introduce dairy products like yogurt and cheese?

Yes, unless otherwise directed by your pediatrician, it is okay to introduce yogurt, cottage cheese, and hard cheeses. Make sure to buy whole milk yogurt and cottage cheese. While it's okay to introduce yogurt, you need to wait until your baby is 12 months before giving him actual cow's milk. You can give your baby yogurt before milk, because the milk proteins are broken down by the culturing process, making them easier to digest. Only hard cheeses are safe to introduce at this stage. These include cheddar and parmesan. It is not safe to introduce soft cheeses at this stage.

Should I continue to feed my baby foods from the 4–6 month age range?

Yes, absolutely. They can be served on their own with a new mushy mash consistency and can also be incorporated into your baby's expanding menu.

For example:
* Mashed banana is absolutely delicious mixed with cherries and quinoa.
* Ripe, juicy pears can now be pureed without cooking and taste great mixed with blueberry puree and yogurt.
* Sweet potato and apple puree can now be mixed with chicken.
* Butternut squash adds a smooth, yummy flavor to lentils.

What should I use to thin lamb, pork and poultry purees?

You can use purified water, breast milk, formula, chicken stock, or vegetable stock to thin these purees. I prefer to use stock, because it adds more flavor. While you can definitely make your own, I prefer to use pre-made, organic, low-sodium stocks. They are available in most markets and grocery store chains. I like to use them because they are full of flavor, low in sodium, and save you the time of having to make your own. Look for stocks that come in boxes rather than cans. Check the ingredient list to make sure the stock is all-natural and preservative-free. Many markets even make their own homemade stock; they are usually kept in the refrigerated section of the store. If you can't find a low-sodium stock, take a small amount of regular stock and dilute it with purified water.

Should I be offering my baby water or juice with her meals?

During mealtime, your baby will be getting enough water in her breast milk or formula to keep her hydrated. However, it's never too early to start drinking water. Try offering your baby a little purified water in her bottle when you're outside on a warm day or when she isn't feeling well and needs extra hydration.

It's not a good idea to offer your baby juice at this stage—it is full of sugar, empty calories, and is not good for her new teeth. However, infused waters have no added sugar, but add that extra hint of flavor your baby, and the rest of your family, will really enjoy. See page 208 for my refreshing infused water recipes.

My baby is teething, what are some healthy alternatives to plastic teething toys?

When your baby is teething she may be cranky or in a lot of discomfort, and therefore not have much of an appetite. It's best to stick with comforting foods like apple, banana, and sweet potato if she's having a bad day. Signs that your baby is teething include, drooling, a low grade fever, wanting to chew on everything, and putting her hands in her mouth.

Semi-frozen fruit purees can be really soothing on your baby's gums. Take one of your fruit purees out of the freezer and let it thaw for a few hours in the refrigerator. Scrape a little off the top with a spoon and let your baby swish the cool puree around in her mouth. The cool sensation is really soothing especially if her gums are swollen.

When babies are teething, they love to bite on things. A good alternative to plastic teething toys are frozen washcloths. Take a clean washcloth, wet a corner, and put it in the freezer for a few hours. Your baby will love chomping down on the frozen corner. Teething biscuits can also provide relief, but they can be a choking hazard if your baby bites off too big of a piece. Never leave your baby unattended when she is noshing on a teething biscuit. Teething rings and toys that are BPA, lead, phthalate and PVC free are another good option.

While teething really hits some babies hard, others have a relatively painless experience. My son Royce got 4 teeth overnight and then, a few weeks later, 6 more teeth came in overnight. It didn't seem to bother him at all. Brendan, on the other hand, had a really rough time. His teeth came in painfully slow—one by one.

7–9 MONTHS

How will I know my baby is ready for finger foods?

At some point during this stage you will notice your baby reaching for her food or trying to grab her spoon. This is most likely her way of letting you know she wants to try and feed herself. Of course she won't be ready to expertly use her spoon for a while yet, but she is ready to start experimenting with finger foods. A great way to start is to sprinkle a few pieces of low sugar "o" cereal on her tray during mealtime. Oat cereal is a perfect starter finger food, because, while your baby will be able to gum it and practice chewing, it will also dissolve in her mouth, so it doesn't pose a choking hazard. However, you should never leave your baby unattended when she is eating.

What are the appropriate finger foods for this stage?

* Low sugar "o" cereal
* Bite sized pieces of ripe, soft fruit, such as banana, pear, avocado, or peach
* Bite size pieces of *cooked* apple
* Bite size pieces of cooked veggies like butternut squash, carrot, zucchini, and parsnips
* Teething biscuits or crackers (be careful your baby doesn't bite off too big of a piece, choking hazard!)

CHOKING HAZARDS! Do not give your baby these foods at this stage:

* Pieces of hot dog
* raisins
* jelly beans
* nuts
* popcorn
* soft bread
* pretzel pieces
* hard raw fruits and veggies like carrots, apples and grapes

Never leave your child unattended when he or she is eating.

Babies love being on the floor. Make sure to wash his/her hands before giving any finger food.

GOOD SOURCE OF:
VITAMIN C
VITAMIN A
FIBER
POTASSIUM
NIACIN
VITAMIN E
VITAMIN K
COPPER
MANGANESE

ALSO CONTAINS:
MAGNESIUM
PHOSPHORUS
PANTOTHENIC ACID
THIAMIN
RIBOFLAVIN
PROTEIN
VITAMIN B6
IRON
FOLATE
ZINC
CALCIUM

SUITABLE FOR
REFRIGERATOR
AND FREEZER

peach

3 Peaches = 6 oz puree

* Wash peaches thoroughly under cold running water, *peel, cut in half, remove and discard pits.
* Chop peaches and place in steamer basket.
* Steam for 3–5 minutes until tender (10 minutes if using frozen peaches).
* Puree into a mushy mash using an immersion blender or food processor. Peaches are naturally juicy so you won't need additional liquid for thinning.
* Let cool and serve or store.
* Peach puree can be stored in Sage Spoonfuls jars for up to 3 days in the refrigerator or up to 3 months in the freezer.
* To peel: cut an X on the bottom of each peach, submerge in boiling water, let boil for 1 minute, remove from water using a slotted spoon, let cool for 2 minutes, and peel the skin off.
* **No-cook puree!** If the peaches are soft and ripe, they can be pureed without steaming

Serving
Peach puree tastes great warm or cool. For a creamier consistency with added nutrition, mix puree with a little breast milk or formula and a baby cereal or grain (rice, oatmeal, barley, amaranth, or quinoa) and serve warm. Add a pinch of cinnamon, nutmeg, or ginger for extra flavor. Peach puree can also be mixed with yogurt or cottage cheese.

On-The-Go
Stored in Sage Spoonfuls jars, peach puree will stay fresh in your cooler, with the frozen ice pack, for up to 12 hours and out of the refrigerator or cooler for up to 2 hours (1 hour out of refrigerator or cooler when mixed with yogurt or cottage cheese).

All About Peach
Peaches have a smooth, velvety texture and a sweet taste that babies love. Plus, they are a good source of disease-fighting carotenes. Buy organic peaches whenever possible, because conventionally grown have high levels of pesticide residue. Look for peaches with smooth skin that gives slightly when squeezed. Under ripe peaches will ripen at room temperature within a day or so. Ripe peaches will stay fresh in the refrigerator for about 3 days. Frozen peaches are great to use when fresh are out of season.

Yummy Combinations With Peach

With Fruit

Peach and Avocado
Peach and Mango
Peach and Banana
Peach and Plum
Peach and Cherry

Peach and Blueberry
Peach, Mango, and Blueberry
Peach, Blueberry, and Banana
Peach, Plum, and Blueberry
Peach, Banana, and Cherry

Combine purees in equal parts. They taste great warm or cool. Try mixing yummy combo with a little breast milk or formula and a baby cereal or grain (rice, oatmeal, amaranth, or quinoa) and serve warm. With the exception of avocado, add a pinch of cinnamon, nutmeg, or ginger for extra flavor. These combos can also be mixed with yogurt or cottage cheese. They will stay fresh in your cooler, with the frozen ice pack, for 12 hours and out of the refrigerator or cooler for 2 hours (1 hour when mixed with yogurt or cottage cheese).

With Vegetables And Beans

Peach and Parsnip
Peach and Pumpkin
Peach and Butternut Squash
Peach and Black Bean

Peach and Sweet Potato
Peach and Cauliflower
Peach and Carrot
Peach, Black Bean, and Tomato

Combine purees in equal parts. They taste great warm and cool. Try mixing yummy combo with a little breast milk or formula and a baby cereal or grain (rice, millet, barley, amaranth, or quinoa) and serve warm. They will stay fresh in your cooler, with the frozen ice pack, for 12 hours and out of the refrigerator or cooler for 2 hours.

With Meat

Peach and Chicken, Pork, Lamb, or Turkey
Peach, Sweet Potato, and Chicken, Pork, Lamb, or Turkey
Peach, Butternut Squash, and Chicken, Pork, Lamb, or Turkey
Peach, Banana, and Chicken, Pork, Lamb, or Turkey

Combine purees in equal parts. They should be served warm. Try mixing yummy combo with a little breast milk, formula or stock and a baby cereal or grain (rice, barley, millet, amaranth, or quinoa). These combos should not be out of the refrigerator for more than 1 hour.

cherries

25 Cherries = 4 oz puree

* Wash cherries thoroughly under cold running water, cut in half, remove and discard pits.
* Place cherries in steamer basket and steam for 3–5 minutes (10 minutes for frozen cherries).
* Puree into a mushy mash using an an immersion blender or food processor. Add cooking water, breast milk, or formula, as needed, to thin puree.
* Let cool and serve or store.
* Cherry puree can be stored in Sage Spoonfuls jars for up to 3 days in the refrigerator or up to 3 months in the freezer.
* **No cook puree!** Cherries can be pureed without steaming, if desired.

Serving
Cherry puree can be served warm or cool. It is a little too sweet on its own and tastes best when mixed with other food. For a creamier consistency with added nutrition, mix puree with a little breast milk or formula and a baby cereal or grain (rice, oatmeal, barley, amaranth, or quinoa) and serve warm. Add a pinch of cinnamon, nutmeg, or ginger for extra flavor. Cherry puree can also be mixed with yogurt or cottage cheese.

On-The-Go
Stored in Sage Spoonfuls jars, cherry puree will stay fresh in your cooler, with the frozen ice pack, for up to 12 hours and out of the refrigeratoror cooler for up to 2 hours (1 hour out of the refrigerator or cooler when mixed with yogurt or cottage cheese).

All About Cherries
Look for sweet cherries—Bing, Lambert, and Rainier varieties are the most popular. Avoid sour cherry varieties. The darker the cherry, the more flavonoid and antioxidant-rich it is. Cherries can boost the immune system and help when your baby is constipated. They are in season and at the peak of sweetness in the summer. Frozen cherries are great to use the rest of the year. Cherries do not continue to ripen once they are picked; look for ones that are firm and plump with shiny skin. They will stay fresh in a plastic bag in the refrigerator for about a week. Cherries stain, take care when preparing and serving.

GOOD SOURCE OF:
VITAMIN C
FIBER
POTASSIUM

ALSO CONTAINS:
MANGANESE
COPPER
VITAMIN K
MAGNESIUM
RIBOFLAVIN
VITAMIN B6
IRON
PHOSPHORUS
PANTOTHENIC ACID
PROTEIN
VITAMIN A
THIAMIN
CALCIUM
NIACIN
FOLATE
ZINC

SUITABLE FOR
REFRIGERATOR
AND FREEZER

Yummy Combinations With Cherries

With Fruit

Cherry and Banana
Cherry and Apple
Cherry and Pear
Cherry and Peach
Cherry and Apricot

Cherry and Plum
Cherry, Banana, and Peach
Cherry, Banana, and Plum
Cherry, Banana, and Blueberry
Cherry, Peach, and Blueberry

Combine purees in equal parts. They taste great warm or cool. Try mixing yummy combo with a little breast milk or formula and a baby cereal or grain (rice, oatmeal, amaranth, or quinoa) and serve warm. Add a pinch of cinnamon, nutmeg, or ginger for extra flavor. These combos can also be mixed with yogurt or cottage cheese. They will stay fresh in your cooler, with the frozen ice pack, for 12 hours and out of the refrigerator or cooler for 2 hours (1 hour when mixed with yogurt or cottage cheese).

With Vegetables

Cherry and Parsnip
Cherry and Sweet Potato

Cherry and Butternut Squash
Cherry and Pumpkin

Combine purees in equal parts. They taste great warm or cool. Try mixing yummy combo with a little breast milk or formula and a baby cereal or grain (rice, millet, amaranth, or quinoa). Add a pinch of cinnamon or nutmeg for extra flavor. These combos will stay fresh in your cooler, with the frozen ice pack, for 12 hours and out of the refrigerator or cooler for 2 hours.

With Meat

Cherry and Chicken, Turkey, Pork, or Lamb
Cherry, Pumpkin, and Chicken, Turkey, Pork, or Lamb
Cherry, Sweet Potato, and Chicken, Turkey, Pork, or Lamb
Cherry, Butternut Squash, and Chicken, Turkey, Pork, or Lamb
Cherry, Parsnip, and Chicken, Turkey, Pork, or Lamb
Cherry, Banana, and Chicken, Turkey, Pork, or Lamb

Combine purees in equal parts. They should be served warm. Try mixing puree with a little breast milk, formula or stock and a baby cereal or grain (rice, barley, millet, amaranth, or quinoa). These combos should not be out of the refrigerator for more than 1 hour.

apricot

3 Apricots = 6 oz puree

EXCELLENT SOURCE OF:
VITAMIN A
VITAMIN C

GOOD SOURCE OF:
FIBER
POTASSIUM

ALSO CONTAINS:
VITAMIN E
VITAMIN K
THIAMIN
RIBOFLAVIN
NIACIN
VITAMIN B6
FOLATE
PANTOTHENIC ACID
CALCIUM
IRON
MAGNESIUM
PHOSPHORUS
ZINC
COPPER
MANGANESE

❄
SUITABLE FOR
REFRIGERATOR
AND FREEZER

✳ Wash apricots thoroughly under cold running water, peel, cut in half, remove and discard pits.

✳ Place apricot halves in steamer basket and steam for 3–5 minutes (10 minutes for dried apricots).

✳ Puree into a mushy mash using an an immersion blender or food processor. Add cooking water, breast milk, or formula, as needed, to thin puree. Puree dried apricots in a food processor only.

✳ Let cool and serve or store.

✳ Apricot puree can be stored in Sage Spoonfuls jars for up to 3 days in the refrigerator or up to 3 months in the freezer.

✳ **No-cook puree!** If the apricots are soft and ripe, they can be pureed without steaming.

Serving
Apricot puree can be served warm or cool. It can be a little tart on its own and tastes best when mixed with other food. Try mixing puree with a little breast milk or formula and a baby cereal or grain (rice, oatmeal, amaranth, or quinoa) and serve warm. For extra flavor, add a pinch of cinnamon, nutmeg, or ginger. Apricot puree can also be mixed with yogurt or cottage cheese.

On-The-Go
Stored in Sage Spoonfuls jars, apricot puree will stay fresh in your cooler, with the frozen ice pack, for up to 12 hours and out of the refrigerator or cooler for up to 2 hours (1 hour out of refrigerator or cooler when mixed with yogurt or cottage cheese).

All About Apricot
Dried apricots are rich in iron and disease-fighting carotenes. The nutrients become concentrated during the drying process which is why dried apricots are more nutrient-dense than fresh. Look for apricots that are dried naturally by the sun and not with sulfur dioxide or other chemicals. Fresh apricots should have a nice golden orange color and give slightly when squeezed. When stored in the refrigerator, whole apricots will stay fresh for about a week.

Yummy Combinations With Apricot

With Fruit

Apricot and Banana	Apricot, Apple, and Pear
Apricot and Apple	Apricot, Banana, and Mango
Apricot and Blueberry	Apricot, Banana, and Blueberry
Apricot and Plum	Apricot, Banana, and Plum
Apricot and Cherry	Apricot, Banana, and Cherry

Combine these purees in equal parts. They taste great warm or cool. Try mixing yummy combo with a little breast milk or formula and a baby cereal or grain (rice, oatmeal, amaranth, or quinoa) and serve warm. Add a pinch of cinnamon, nutmeg, or ginger for extra flavor. These combos can also be mixed with yogurt or cottage cheese. They will stay fresh in your cooler, with the frozen ice pack, for 12 hours and out of the refrigerator or cooler for 2 hours (1 hour when mixed with yogurt or cottage cheese).

With Vegetables

Apricot and Sweet Potato	Apricot and Carrot
Apricot and Parsnip	Apricot and Cauliflower
Apricot and Butternut Squash	Apricot, Banana, and Parsnip
Apricot and Pumpkin	Apricot, Banana, and Pumpkin

Combine purees in equal parts. They taste great warm and cool. Try mixing yummy combo with a little breast milk or formula and a baby cereal or grain (rice, barley, millet, amaranth, or quinoa) and serve warm. Add a pinch of cinnamon, nutmeg, or ginger for extra flavor. They will stay fresh in your cooler, with the frozen ice pack, for 12 hours and out of the refrigerator or cooler for 2 hours.

With Meat

Apricot and Chicken, Lamb, Pork, or Turkey
Apricot, Sweet Potato, and Chicken, Lamb, Pork, or Turkey
Apricot, Butternut Squash, and Chicken, Lamb, Pork, or Turkey
Apricot, Parsnip, and Chicken, Lamb, Pork, or Turkey
Apricot, Banana, and Chicken, Lamb, Pork, or Turkey

Combine purees in equal parts. They should be served warm. Try mixing yummy combo with a little breast milk, formula or stock, and a baby cereal or grain (rice, millet, barley, amaranth, or quinoa). These combos should not be out of the refrigerator for more than 1 hour.

plum

3 Plums = 6 oz puree

7–9 MONTHS AND UP

EXCELLENT SOURCE OF:
VITAMIN C

GOOD SOURCE OF:
VITAMIN K
VITAMIN A
FIBER
POTASSIUM

ALSO CONTAINS:
COPPER
MANGANESE
THIAMIN
RIBOFLAVIN
NIACIN
MAGNESIUM
PHOSPHORUS
VITAMIN E
VITAMIN B6
FOLATE
PANTOTHENIC ACID
IRON
PROTEIN
CALCIUM
ZINC

SUITABLE FOR REFRIGERATOR AND FREEZER

✳ Wash plums thoroughly under cold running water, peel, cut in half, remove, and discard pits.

✳ Chop plum, place in steamer basket and steam for 3–5 minutes.

✳ Puree into a mushy mash using an an immersion blender or food processor. Plums are naturally juicy, so you won't need additional liquid to thin puree.

✳ Let cool and serve or store.

✳ Plum puree can be stored in Sage Spoonfuls jars for up to 3 days in refrigerator or up to 3 months in freezer.

✳ **No-cook puree!** If the plums are soft and ripe, they can be pureed without steaming.

Serving
Plum puree can be served warm or cool. Sweet black plum puree can be served on its own, but other plums can be a little tart and taste best when mixed with other food. For a creamier consistency with added nutrition, mix puree with a little breast milk or formula and a baby cereal or grain (rice, oatmeal, aramanth, or quinoa) and serve warm. Add a pinch of cinnamon, nutmeg, or ginger for extra flavor. Plum puree can also be mixed with yogurt or cottage cheese.

On-The-Go
Stored in Sage Spoonfuls jars, plum puree will stay fresh in your cooler, with the frozen ice pack, for up to 12 hours and out of the refrigerator or cooler for up to 2 hours (1 hour out of refrigerator or cooler when mixed with yogurt or cottage cheese).

All About Plum
Black plums are the sweetest variety while yellow and red can be a little tart. Plums are rich in antioxidants. They are also a good source of fiber and can be helpful when your baby is constipated. Look for plums that have smooth skin and give a little when squeezed. Under ripe plums will ripen at room temperature in a day or two. Ripe plums will stay fresh in the refrigerator for about 3 days.

Yummy Combinations With Plum

With Fruit

Plum and Apple
Plum and Banana
Plum and Peach
Plum and Pear

Plum, Banana, and Peach
Plum, Banana, and Blueberry
Plum, Banana, and Cherry
Plum, Peach, and Banana

Combine purees in equal parts. They taste great warm or cool. Try mixing yummy combo with a little breast milk or formula and a baby cereal or grain (rice, oatmeal, amaranth, or quinoa) and serve warm. Add a pinch of cinnamon, nutmeg, or ginger for extra flavor. These combos can also be mixed with yogurt or cottage cheese. They will stay fresh in your cooler, with the frozen ice pack, for 12 hours and out of the refrigerator or cooler for 2 hours (1 hour when mixed with yogurt or cottage cheese).

With Vegetables

Plum and Parsnip
Plum and Butternut Squash
Plum and Cauliflower

Plum and Pumpkin
Plum and Sweet Potato
Plum and Carrot

Combine purees in equal parts. They taste great warm or cool. Try mixing yummy combo with a little breast milk or formula and a baby cereal or grain (rice, barley, millet, amaranth, or quinoa) and serve warm. These combos will stay fresh in your cooler, with the frozen ice pack, for 12 hours and out of the refrigerator or cooler for 2 hours.

With Meat

Plum and Chicken, Pork, Lamb, or Turkey
Plum, Sweet Potato, and Chicken, Pork, Lamb, or Turkey
Plum, Butternut Squash, and Chicken, Pork, Lamb, or Turkey
Plum, Banana, and Chicken, Pork, Lamb, or Turkey

Combine purees in equal parts. They should be served warm. Try mixing yummy combo with a little breast milk, formula or stock and a baby cereal or grain (rice, barley, millet, amaranth, or quinoa). These combos should not be out of the refrigerator for more than 1 hour.

7–9 MONTHS

mango

1 Mango = 6 oz puree

* Peel mango, cut the fruit away from the pit and chop.
* Place mango in a steamer basket and steam for 3–5 minutes (10 minutes if using frozen).
* Puree into a mushy mash using an an immersion blender or food processor. Mangoes are very juicy, so you won't need additional liquid to thin puree.
* Let cool and serve or store.
* Mango puree can be stored in Sage Spoonfuls jars for up to 3 days in the refrigerator or up to 3 months in the freezer.
* **No-cook puree!** If the mango is soft and ripe, it can be pureed without steaming.

EXCELLENT SOURCE OF:
VITAMIN C
VITAMIN A

GOOD SOURCE OF:
FIBER
VITAMIN B6
VITAMIN E
VITAMIN K
COPPER
POTASSIUM
THIAMIN
RIBOFLAVIN
NIACIN
FOLATE

ALSO CONTAINS:
PANTOTHENIC ACID
CALCIUM
IRON
MAGNESIUM
PHOSPHORUS
MANGANESE
SELENIUM
PROTEIN

SUITABLE FOR
REFRIGERATOR
AND FREEZER

Serving
Mango puree can be served warm or cool. It is a little tart on its own and tastes best when mixed with other food. Try mixing puree with a little breast milk or formula and a baby cereal or grain (rice, oatmeal, or quinoa) and serve warm. For extra flavor, add a pinch of ginger. Mango puree is also delicious when mixed with yogurt or cottage cheese.

On-The-Go
Stored in Sage Spoonfuls jars, mango puree will stay fresh in your cooler, with the frozen ice pack, for up to 12 hours and out of the refrigerator or cooler for up to 2 hours (1 hour out of refrigerator or cooler when mixed with yogurt or cottage cheese).

All About Mango
Mangoes are a deliciously sweet, easy to digest, and widely available tropical fruit. They are packed with nutrients and disease-fighting antioxidants. Mango puree is full of fiber and can be helpful when your baby is constipated. It can also be helpful when your baby has an upset stomach. Look for mangoes that have a smooth orange/red skin and give a little when squeezed. Allow under ripe mangoes to ripen at room temperature for a few days. Whole mangoes will stay fresh at room temperature for about 1 week. If fresh mangoes are unavailable, frozen are great to use as well.

Yummy Combinations With Mango

With Fruit

Mango and Banana
Mango and Blueberry
Mango and Cantaloupe
Mango and Avocado
Mango, Banana, and Plum

Mango, Apricot, and Banana
Mango, Banana, and Peach
Mango, Banana, and Blueberry
Mango, Peach, and Blueberry
Mango, Cherry, and Banana

Combine purees in equal parts. They taste great warm or cool. Try mixing yummy combo with a little breast milk or formula and a baby cereal or grain (rice, oatmeal, aramanth, or quinoa) and serve warm. With the exception of avocado, add a pinch of ginger for added flavor. These combos can also be mixed with yogurt or cottage cheese. They will stay fresh in your cooler, with the frozen ice pack, for 12 hours and out of the refrigerator or cooler for 2 hours (1 hour when mixed with yogurt or cottage cheese).

With Vegetables And Beans

Mango and Parsnip
Mango and Cauliflower
Mango and Sweet Potato
Mango and Butternut Squash

Mango and Pumpkin
Mango and Carrot
Mango and Black Bean
Mango, Carrot, and Parsnip

Combine purees in equal parts. They taste great warm or cool. Try mixing yummy combo with breast milk or formula and a baby cereal or grain (rice, millet, barley, quinoa, or amaranth) and serve warm. They will stay fresh in your cooler, with the frozen ice pack, for 12 hours and out of the refrigerator or cooler for 2 hours.

With Meat

Mango and Chicken, Pork, Lamb, or Turkey
Mango, Black Bean, and Chicken or Turkey
Mango, Parsnip, and Chicken, Pork, Lamb, or Turkey
Mango, Banana, and Chicken, Pork, Lamb, or Turkey
Mango, Butternut Squash, and Chicken, Pork, Lamb, or Turkey

Combine purees in equal parts. They should be served warm. Try mixing yummy combo with a little breast milk, formula, or stock and a baby cereal or grain (rice, millet, barley, amaranth, or quinoa). Add a pinch of fresh parsley for extra flavor. These combos should not be out of the refrigerator for more than 1 hour.

EXCELLENT SOURCE OF:
VITAMIN K
FIBER
POTASSIUM
VITAMIN A
MANGANESE
COPPER

GOOD SOURCE OF:
RIBOFLAVIN
VITAMIN B6
MAGNESIUM
NIACIN
PHOSPHORUS
IRON
PROTEIN
CALCIUM
PANTOTHENIC ACID
THIAMIN

ALSO CONTAINS:
ZINC
VITAMIN E
VITAMIN C
FOLATE
SELENIUM

❄
SUITABLE FOR
REFRIGERATOR
AND FREEZER

prune

1 Cup of Prunes = 4 oz puree

* Place prunes in a steamer basket and steam for about 10 minutes until tender.

* Puree into a mushy mash using using a food processor. Prune puree can be pasty and sticky; add cooking water, breast milk or formula, as needed, to thin puree.

* Let cool and serve or store.

* Prunes can be stored in Sage Spoonfuls jars for up to 3 days in the refrigerator or up to 3 months in the freezer.

Serving
Prune puree can be served warm or cool. A little of this puree goes a long way. For a creamier consistency with added nutrition, mix puree with a little breast milk or formula and a baby cereal (rice, oatmeal, amaranth or quinoa) and serve warm. Add a pinch of cinnamon for extra flavor. Prune puree can also be mixed with yogurt or cottage cheese.

On-The-Go
Stored in Sage Spoonfuls jars, prune puree will stay fresh in your cooler, with the frozen ice pack, for up to 12 hours and out of the refrigerator or cooler for up to 2 hours (1 hour out of refrigerator or cooler when mixed with yogurt or cottage cheese).

All About Prune
Prunes are dried plums. They are full of nutrients and antioxidants. Prunes are a natural laxative and can be helpful when your baby is constipated. Be sure to buy prunes that were sun-dried and not dried with sulphur dioxide or other chemicals. When stored in an airtight container in the refrigerator, prunes will stay fresh for up to 6 months.

Yummy Combinations With Prune

With Fruit

Prune and Pear
Prune and Peach
Prune and Banana
Prune and Apple

Prune, Banana, and Peach
Prune, Banana, and Pear
Prune, Banana, and Blueberry
Prune, Banana, and Mango

Combine a small amount of prune puree with a larger portion of the other purees. They taste great warm or cool. Try mixing yummy combo with a little breast milk or formula and a baby cereal or grain (rice, oatmeal, amaranth, or quinoa) and serve warm. Add a pinch of cinnamon, nutmeg, or ginger for extra flavor. These combos can also be mixed with yogurt or cottage cheese. They will stay fresh in your cooler, with the frozen ice pack, for 12 hours and out of the refrigerator or cooler for 2 hours (1 hour when mixed with yogurt or cottage cheese).

With Vegetables

Prune and Butternut Squash
Prune and Carrot
Prune and Parsnip
Prune and Pumpkin

Prune and Sweet Potato
Prune, Apple, and Butternut Squash
Prune, Carrot, and Butternut Squash
Prune, Apple, and Carrot

Combine a small amount of prune puree with a larger portion of the other purees. They taste best warm but can also be served cool. Try mixing yummy combo with a little breast milk or formula and a baby cereal or grain (rice, barley, millet, amaranth, or quinoa) and serve warm. Add a pinch of cinnamon, nutmeg, or ginger for extra flavor. They will stay fresh in your cooler, with the frozen ice pack, for 12 hours and out of the refrigerator or cooler for 2 hours.

With Meat

Prune and Lamb, Chicken, Pork, or Turkey
Prune, Butternut Squash, and Lamb, Chicken, Pork, or Turkey
Prune, Sweet Potato, and Lamb, Chicken, Pork, or Turkey

Combine a small amount of prune puree with a larger portion of the other purees. They should be served warm. Try mixing yummy combo with a little breast milk, formula, or stock and a baby cereal or grain (rice, millet, barley, amaranth, or quinoa). These combos should not be out of the refrigerator for more than 1 hour.

blueberries

1 Cup of Blueberries = 4 oz puree

EXCELLENT SOURCE OF:
VITAMIN K
MANGANESE
VITAMIN C

GOOD SOURCE OF:
FIBER

ALSO CONTAINS:
VITAMIN E
THIAMIN
RIBOFLAVIN
VITAMIN B6
COPPER
NIACIN
POTASSIUM
VITAMIN A
FOLATE
PANTOTHENIC ACID
IRON
MAGNESIUM
PHOSPHORUS
ZINC
PROTEIN
CALCIUM

SUITABLE FOR
REFRIGERATOR
AND FREEZER

* Place blueberries in a strainer and wash thoroughly under cold running water.

* Put them in a steamer basket and steam for about 3 minutes (7 minutes if using frozen).

* Puree using an immersion blender or food processor. Blueberry puree has more of a syrupy consistency than a mushy mash. If desired, place blueberry puree into a strainer, placed over a bowl, and push it through the strainer with a spatula or spoon to remove skins.

* Let cool and serve or store.

* Blueberry puree can be stored in Sage Spoonfuls jars for up to 3 days in the refrigerator or up to 3 months in the freezer.

* **No-cook puree!** Fresh blueberries can be pureed without steaming, if desired.

Serving
Blueberry puree can be served warm or cool. It has a syrupy consistency and is best mixed with other food. For a creamier consistency with added nutrition, mix puree with a little breast milk or formula and a baby cereal or grain (rice, oatmeal, amaranth or quinoa) and serve warm. Add a pinch of cinnamon for extra flavor. Blueberry puree can also be mixed with yogurt or cottage cheese.

On-The-Go
Stored in Sage Spoonfuls jars, blueberry puree will stay fresh in your cooler, with the frozen ice pack, for up to 12 hours and out of the refrigerator or cooler for up to 2 hours (1 hour out of refrigerator or cooler when mixed with yogurt or cottage cheese).

All About Blueberries
Blueberries contain the highest levels of disease-fighting antioxidants of any fruit or vegetable, and make a great staple food in your baby's diet. Additionally, they can be helpful with constipation and diarrhea. Look for blueberries that are firm to the touch, with a rich deep blue color. They will stay fresh in your refrigerator for up to 1 week. Frozen blueberries are a great choice when fresh are out of season. Buy organic blueberries whenever possible. Blueberries stain—take care when preparing and serving.

Yummy Combinations With Blueberries

With Fruit

Blueberry and Banana
Blueberry and Peach
Blueberry and Apple
Blueberry and Pear
Blueberry and Apricot
Blueberry and Cantaloupe
Blueberry and Mango
Blueberry and Cherry

Blueberry Peach, and Pear
Blueberry, Banana, and Peach
Blueberry, Banana, and Mango
Blueberry, Apple, and Banana
Blueberry, Banana, and Apricot
Blueberry, Peach, and Mango
Blueberry, Banana, and Cherry
Blueberry, Banana, and Plum

Combine purees in equal parts. They taste great warm or cool. Try mixing yummy combo with a little breast milk or formula and a baby cereal or grain (rice, oatmeal, amaranth, or quinoa) and serve warm. Add a pinch of cinnamon, nutmeg, or ginger for extra flavor. They can also be mixed with yogurt or cottage cheese. These combos will stay fresh in your cooler, with the frozen ice pack, for 12 hours and out of the refrigerator or cooler for 2 hours (1 hour when mixed with yogurt or cottage cheese).

With Vegetables

Blueberry and Parsnip
Blueberry and Carrot
Blueberry and Pumpkin
Blueberry and Sweet Potato
Blueberry and Butternut Squash

Blueberry, Pumpkin, and Pear
Blueberry, Sweet Potato, and Apple
Blueberry, Butternut Squash, and Apple
Blueberry, Butternut Squash, and Pear
Blueberry, Pumpkin, and Apple

Combine purees in equal parts. They taste great warm or cool. Try mixing yummy combo with a little breast milk or formula and a baby cereal or grain (rice, barley, millet, amaranth, or quinoa) and serve warm. Add a pinch of cinnamon, nutmeg, or ginger for extra flavor. These combos will stay fresh in your cooler, with the frozen ice pack, for 12 hours and out of the refrigerator or cooler for 2 hours.

7-9 MONTHS

cantaloupe

½ Medium Cantaloupe = 14 oz puree

EXCELLENT SOURCE OF:
VITAMIN A
VITAMIN C
VITAMIN B6
POTASSIUM

GOOD SOURCE OF:
FOLATE
FIBER
VITAMIN K
NIACIN
THIAMIN
MAGNESIUM
PANTOTHENIC ACID

ALSO CONTAINS:
COPPER
MANGANESE
PROTEIN
PHOSPHORUS
RIBOFLAVIN
CALCIUM
IRON
ZINC
SODIUM
SELENIUM

SUITABLE FOR
REFRIGERATOR
AND FREEZER

* Wash the whole melon thoroughly under cold running water. This will remove any germs from the rind that could transfer onto the melon during preparation.

* Cut the cantaloupe in half, scoop out and discard the seeds. Store the remaining ½ cantaloupe in the refrigerator in an air tight container.

* Cut the half in half and slice the fruit off of rind. Discard rinds.

* Chop cantaloupe, place in steamer basket, and steam for 3–5 minutes.

* Puree into a mushy mash using an an immersion blender or food processor. Cantaloupe is naturally very juicy, so you won't need additional liquid to thin puree.

* Let cool and serve or store.

* Cantaloupe puree can be stored in Sage Spoonfuls jars for up to 3 days in the refrigerator and up to 3 months in freezer.

* **No-cook puree!** Cantaloupe can be pureed without steaming, if desired.

Serving
Cantaloupe puree can be served warm or cool. For a creamier consistency with added nutrition, mix puree with a little breast milk or formula and a baby cereal or grain (rice, oatmeal, amaranth, or quinoa) and serve warm. Cantaloupe puree can also be mixed with yogurt or cottage cheese.

On-The-Go
Stored in Sage Spoonfuls jars, cantaloupe puree will stay fresh in your cooler, with the frozen ice pack, for up to 12 hours and out of the refrigerator or cooler for up to 2 hours (1 hour out of refrigerator or cooler when mixed with yogurt or cottage cheese).

All About Cantaloupe
Cantaloupes are the most nutrient rich melon variety. They are juicy, sweet, and have a velvety texture. Cantaloupe puree is a good source of fiber and can be helpful when your baby is constipated. Semi-frozen cantaloupe puree can be soothing to a baby's gums when teething. One of the sure signs of a ripe cantaloupe is if you can smell the sweetness of the melon through the rind. Ripe cantaloupes will stay fresh at room temperature for about 5 days. Under ripe cantaloupes will ripen at room temperature within a few days.

Yummy Combinations With Cantaloupe

With Fruit

Cantaloupe and Banana
Cantaloupe and Mango
Cantaloupe and Pear
Cantaloupe and Peach

Cantaloupe, Banana, and Peach
Cantaloupe, Banana, and Blueberry
Cantaloupe, Mango, and Blueberry
Cantaloupe, Cherry, and Plum

Combine purees in equal parts. They taste great warm or cool. Try mixing yummy combo with a little breast milk or formula and a baby cereal or grain (rice, oatmeal, amaranth, or quinoa) and serve warm. Add a pinch of cinnamon, nutmeg, or ginger for extra flavor. These combos can also be mixed with yogurt or cottage cheese. They will stay fresh in your cooler, with the frozen ice pack, for 12 hours and out of the refrigerator or cooler for 2 hours (1 hour when mixed with yogurt or cottage cheese).

With Vegetables And Beans

Cantaloupe and Parsnip
Cantaloupe and Carrot
Cantaloupe and Lentil
Cantaloupe and Sweet Potato

Cantaloupe and Pumpkin
Cantaloupe and Cauliflower
Cantaloupe and Black Bean
Cantaloupe and Butternut Squash

Combine purees in equal parts. They taste great warm or cool. Try mixing yummy combo with a little breast milk or formula and a baby cereal or grain (rice, barley, millet, amaranth, or quinoa) and serve warm. These combos will stay fresh in your cooler, with the frozen ice pack, for 12 hours and out of the refrigerator or cooler for 2 hours.

With Meat

Cantaloupe and Chicken, Pork, Turkey, or Lamb
Cantaloupe, Butternut Squash, and Chicken, Pork, Turkey, or Lamb
Cantaloupe, Sweet Potato, and Chicken, Pork, Turkey, or Lamb

Combine puree in equal parts. They should be served warm. Try mixing yummy combo with a little breast milk, formula, or stock and a baby cereal or grain (rice, barley, millet, amaranth, or quinoa). These combos should not be out of the refrigerator for more than 1 hour.

7–9 MONTHS

green beans

½ Pound of Green Beans = 8 oz puree

EXCELLENT SOURCE OF:
VITAMIN C
VITAMIN K
VITAMIN A
FIBER

GOOD SOURCE OF:
MANGANESE
FOLATE
RIBOFLAVIN
MAGNESIUM
POTASSIUM
IRON
THIAMIN
PHOSPHORUS
PROTEIN
CARBOHYDRATES

ALSO CONTAINS:
NIACIN
VITAMIN B6
CALCIUM
COPPER
VITAMIN E
ZINC
PANTOTHENIC ACID
SELENIUM

SUITABLE FOR
REFRIGERATOR
AND FREEZER

* Wash green beans thoroughly under cold running water, snap or cut off ends and discard.
* Cut beans in half and place in steamer basket.
* Steam for 5–7 minutes until bright green and tender (10 minutes if using frozen).
* Puree into a mushy mash using an an immersion blender or food processor. Add cooking water, breast milk, formula, or stock, as needed, to thin puree.
* Let cool and serve or store.
* Green beans can be stored in Sage Spoonfuls jars for up to 3 days in the refrigerator or up to 3 months in the freezer.

Serving
Green bean puree tastes great warm or cool. Try mixing puree with a little breast milk, formula or stock and a baby cereal or grain (rice, barley, millet, amaranth, or quinoa). Add a pinch of fresh mint or grated cheese for extra flavor.

On-The-Go
Stored in Sage Spoonfuls jars, green bean puree will stay fresh in your cooler, with the frozen ice pack, for up to 12 hours and out of the refrigerator or cooler for up to 2 hours.

All About Green Beans
Green beans have a mild taste and are a good source of complex carbohydrates and fiber. They have also been shown to promote a healthy heart. Look for green beans that are firm with an even green color. They will stay fresh in the refrigerator for about 1 week. Frozen green beans can also be used.

Yummy Combinations With Green Beans

With Vegetables And Beans

Green Bean and Carrot
Green Bean and Potato
Green Bean and Cauliflower
Green Bean and Zucchini
Green Bean and Parsnip

Green Bean and Butternut Squash
Green Bean and Sweet Potato
Green Bean, Tomato, and Zucchini
Green Bean, Carrot, and Parsnip
Green Bean, Lentil, and Sweet Potato

Combine purees in equal parts. They taste best warm, but can also be served cool. Try mixing yummy combo with a little breast milk, formula, or stock and a baby cereal or grain (rice, barley, millet, amaranth, or quinoa). With the exception of potato/sweet potato, these combos can also be mixed with small shaped pasta. Add a pinch of grated cheese for extra flavor. They will stay fresh in your cooler with, the frozen ice pack, for 12 hours and out of the refrigerator or cooler for 2 hours.

With Meat

Green Bean, Potato, and Chicken, Turkey, Pork, or Lamb
Green Bean, Sweet Potato, and Chicken, Turkey, Pork, or Lamb
Green Bean, Butternut Squash, and Chicken, Turkey, Pork, or Lamb
Green Bean, Parsnip, and Chicken, Turkey, Pork, or Lamb
Green Bean, Carrot, and Chicken, Turkey, Pork, or Lamb

Combine purees in equal parts. They should be served warm. Try mixing puree with a little breast milk, formula, or stock and a baby cereal or grain (rice, barley, millet, amaranth, or quinoa). With the exception of potato/sweet potato, these combos can also be mixed with small shaped pasta. Add a pinch of parsley or grated cheese for extra flavor. These combos should not be out of the refrigerator for more than 1 hour.

leeks

1 Medium Leek = 3 oz puree

* Cut off the root and dark green part of the leek and discard.
* Slice the leek lengthwise and then slice into smaller pieces crosswise.
* Place the leek in a strainer and rinse thoroughly under cold running water to remove all sand and dirt.
* Place leek in steamer basket and steam for about 5 minutes.
* Puree into a mushy mash using a food processor. Add a little breast milk, formula, purified water, or stock, as needed, to thin puree.
* Let cool and serve or store.
* Leek puree can be stored in Sage Spoonfuls jars for up to 3 days in the refrigerator or up to 3 months in the freezer.

Serving
Leek is a member of the onion/garlic family and is best when combined in small quantities with other foods.

On-The-Go
Stored in Sage Spoonfuls jars, leek puree will stay fresh in your cooler, with the frozen ice pack, for up to 12 hours, and out of the refrigerator or cooler for up to 2 hours.

All About Leeks
Leeks are rich in cancer-fighting and immune system-boosting nutrients. Look for leeks that are dark green at the tips and a clean white on the bottom. They will stay fresh in a plastic bag in your refrigerator for 7–10 days.

Yummy Combinations With Leeks

With Vegetables And Beans

Leek and Parsnip
Leek and Potato
Leek and Sweet Potato
Leek and Butternut Squash
Leek, Parsnip, and Carrot
Leek, Broccoli, and Lentil
Leek, Lentil, and Sweet Potato

Leek, Pea, and Potato
Leek, Carrot, and Lentil
Leek, Asparagus, and Potato
Leek, Split Pea, and Parsnip
Leek, Split Pea, and Carrot
Leek, Zucchini, and Potato
Leek, Green Bean, and Sweet Potato

Combine a small amount of leek puree with larger portions of the other purees. These combos taste best warm. Try mixing yummy combo with a little breast milk, formula, or stock and a baby cereal or grain (rice, barley, millet, amaranth, or quinoa). These combos will stay fresh in your cooler, with the frozen ice pack, for 12 hours or out of the refrigerator or cooler for 2 hours.

With Meat

Leek, Pumpkin, and Chicken, Pork, Turkey, or Lamb
Leek, Butternut Squash, and Chicken, Pork, Turkey, or Lamb
Leek, Sweet Potato, and Chicken, Pork, Turkey, or Lamb
Leek, Carrot, Lentil, and Chicken, Pork, Turkey, or Lamb
Leek, Parsnip, and Chicken, Pork, Turkey, or Lamb

Combine a small amount of leek puree with larger portions of the other purees. They should be served warm. Try mixing yummy combo with a little breast milk, formula, or stock and a baby cereal or grain (rice, barley, millet, amaranth, or quinoa). Add a pinch of fresh sage, thyme, or parsley for extra flavor. These combos should not be out of the refrigerator for more than 1 hour.

cauliflower

½ Head of Cauliflower = 15 oz puree

* Wash cauliflower thoroughly under cold running water, remove green leaves and discard.
* Cut cauliflower in half and cut florets from the stem. Store remaining half in a plastic bag in the refrigerator.
* Place florets in steamer basket and steam for 8–10 minutes (10–12 if using frozen).
* Puree into a mushy mash using an immersion blender or food processor. Add cooking water, breast milk, formula, or stock, as needed, to thin puree.
* Let cool and serve or store.
* Cauliflower puree can be stored in Sage Spoonfuls jars for up to 3 days in the refrigerator and up to 3 months in the freezer.

Serving
Cauliflower puree tastes great warm or cool. Try mixing puree with a little breast milk, formula, or stock and a baby cereal or grain (rice, barley, millet, amaranth, or quinoa) and serve warm. Add a pinch of turmeric or grated cheese for extra flavor.

On-The-Go
Stored in Sage Spoonfuls jars, cauliflower puree will stay fresh in your cooler, with the frozen ice pack, for up to 12 hours and out of the refrigerator or cooler for up to 2 hours.

All About Cauliflower
Cauliflower puree combines really well with a number of other foods. It is surprisingly tasty when combined with fruit purees. As a member of the cabbage family, cauliflower is rich in cancer-fighting phytochemicals. Look for cauliflower that has crisp green leaves and white flower heads. Avoid cauliflower that looks wilted or discolored. It will stay fresh in a plastic bag in the refrigerator for up to 1 week. Frozen cauliflower can also be used.

7–9 MONTHS AND UP

EXCELLENT SOURCE OF:
VITAMIN C
VITAMIN K

GOOD SOURCE OF:
FOLATE
VITAMIN B6
FIBER
POTASSIUM
MANGANESE
PANTOTHENIC ACID
PHOSPHORUS

ALSO CONTAINS:
PROTEIN
THIAMIN
RIBOFLAVIN
NIACIN
CALCIUM
IRON
MAGNESIUM
SODIUM
ZINC
COPPER
SELENIUM

SUITABLE FOR
REFRIGERATOR
AND FREEZER

Yummy Combinations With Cauliflower

With Fruit

Cauliflower and Apricot   Cauliflower and Apple
Cauliflower and Pear   Cauliflower and Peach

Combine purees in equal parts. They taste great warm and cool. Try mixing yummy combo with a little breast milk or formula and a baby cereal or grain (rice, millet, amaranth, or quinoa). These combos will stay fresh in your cooler, with the frozen ice pack, for 12 hours and out of the refrigerator or cooler for 2 hours.

With Vegetables

Cauliflower and Green Bean   Cauliflower and Broccoli
Cauliflower and Carrot   Cauliflower and Butternut Squash
Cauliflower and Pea   Cauliflower, Potato and Leek
Cauliflower and Sweet Potato   Cauliflower, Broccoli, and Carrot
Cauliflower and Pumpkin   Cauliflower, Pea, and Carrot
Cauliflower and Zucchini   Cauliflower, Potato, and Carrot

Combine purees in equal parts. They taste best warm, but can also be served cool. Try mixing yummy combo with a little breast milk or formula and a baby cereal or grain (rice, barley, millet, amaranth, or quinoa). Add a pinch of turmeric or grated cheese for extra flavor. These combos can also be mixed with small shaped pasta, with the exception of potato and sweet potato. They will stay fresh in your cooler, with the frozen ice pack, for 12 hours and out of the refrigerator or cooler for 2 hours.

With Meat

Cauliflower and Chicken, Lamb, Pork, or Turkey
Cauliflower, Carrot, and Chicken, Lamb, Pork, or Turkey
Cauliflower, Broccoli, and Chicken, Lamb, Pork, or Turkey
Cauliflower, Sweet Potato, and Chicken, Lamb, Pork, or Turkey
Cauliflower, Butternut Squash, and Chicken, Lamb, Pork, or Turkey

Combine purees in equal parts. They should be served warm. Try mixing yummy combo with a little breast milk, formula, or stock and a baby cereal or grain (rice, millet, barley, amaranth, or quinoa). Add a pinch of fresh parsley, turmeric, ginger, or grated cheese for extra flavor. With the exception of sweet potato, these combos can be mixed with small shaped pasta. They should not be out of the refrigerator for more than 1 hour.

broccoli

1 Head of Broccoli = 14 oz puree

EXCELLENT SOURCE OF:
VITAMIN C
VITAMIN A
VITAMIN K
FOLATE
FIBER

GOOD SOURCE OF:
MANGANESE
POTASSIUM
VITAMIN B6
RIBOFLAVIN
PHOSPHORUS
MAGNESIUM
VITAMIN E

ALSO CONTAINS:
PROTEIN
PANTOTHENIC ACID
THIAMIN
CALCIUM
IRON
SELENIUM
NIACIN
ZINC
COPPER
SODIUM

SUITABLE FOR
REFRIGERATOR
AND FREEZER

* Wash broccoli thoroughly under cold running water, cut into florets and discard rough stem.
* Place broccoli into steamer basket and steam 7–8 minutes (10 minutes if using frozen) until bright green and tender.
* Puree into a mushy mash using an immersion blender or food processor. Add cooking water, breast milk, formula or stock, as needed, to thin puree.
* Let cool and serve or store.
* Broccoli puree can be stored in Sage Spoonfuls jars for up to 3 days in the refrigerator or up to 3 months in the freezer.

Serving
Broccoli tastes best warm, but can also be served cool. Try mixing puree with a little breast milk, formula, or stock and a baby cereal or grain (rice, barley, millet, amaranth, or quinoa). Broccoli can also be mixed with small shaped pasta. Add some grated cheese for extra flavor.

On-The-Go
Stored in Sage Spoonfuls jars, broccoli puree will stay fresh in your cooler, with the frozen ice pack, for up to 12 hours and out of the refrigerator or cooler for up to 2 hours.

All About Broccoli
Broccoli is rich in nutrients, is an excellent source of cancer-fighting phytochemicals, and has been shown to help the liver detoxify chemicals in the body. It also contains lutein, which promotes healthy eyes. Fresh broccoli should have an even, deep green color and firm stalks and stems. It will stay fresh in a plastic bag in the refrigerator for about 5–7 days. Frozen broccoli can be used as well.

Yummy Combinations With Broccoli

With Vegetables

Broccoli and Potato	Broccoli, Potato, and Carrot
Broccoli and Pumpkin	Broccoli, Carrot, and Zucchini
Broccoli and Carrot	Broccoli, Sweet Potato, and Pea
Broccoli and Cauliflower	Broccoli, Cauliflower, and Potato
Broccoli and Sweet Potato	Broccoli, Carrot, and Parsnip
Broccoli and Butternut Squash	Broccoli, Cauliflower, and Sweet Potato

Combine purees in equal parts. They taste best warm, but can also be served cool. Try mixing yummy combo with a little breast milk, formula, or stock and a baby cereal or grain (rice, barley, millet, amaranth, or quinoa). Add a pinch of parsley or grated cheese for extra flavor. With the exception of potato and sweet potato, these combos can also be mixed with small shaped pasta. They will stay fresh in your cooler, with the frozen ice pack, for 12 hours or out of the refrigerator or cooler for 2 hours.

With Meat

Broccoli and Chicken, Turkey, Pork, or Lamb
Broccoli, Sweet Potato, and Chicken, Turkey, Pork, or Lamb
Broccoli, Parsnip, and Chicken, Turkey, Pork, or Lamb
Broccoli, Potato, and Chicken, Turkey, Pork, or Lamb
Broccoli, Carrot, and Chicken, Turkey, Pork, or Lamb

Combine purees in equal parts. They should be served warm. Try mixing yummy combo with a little breast milk, formula, or stock and a baby cereal or grain (rice, barley, millet, amaranth, or quinoa). These combos should not be out of the refrigerator for more than 1 hour.

7–9 MONTHS

asparagus

1 Bunch Fresh Asparagus = 10 oz puree

7–9 MONTHS AND UP

EXCELLENT SOURCE OF:
VITAMIN K
VITAMIN A
FOLATE
VITAMIN C

GOOD SOURCE OF:
IRON
THIAMIN
COPPER
FIBER
RIBOFLAVIN
MANGANESE
VITAMIN E
POTASSIUM
PHOSPHORUS
NIACIN
VITAMIN B6
PROTEIN

ALSO CONTAINS:
MAGNESIUM
ZINC
PANOTHENIC ACID
SELENIUM
CALCIUM

SUITABLE FOR
REFRIGERATOR
AND FREEZER

✳ Wash asparagus thoroughly under cold running water, snap off rough ends, and cut into pieces.

✳ Place asparagus in steamer basket and steam for about 5 minutes, until bright green and tender (10 minutes if using frozen).

✳ Puree into a mushy mash using an immersion blender or food processor. You will not need additional liquid for thinning.

✳ Let cool and serve or store.

✳ Asparagus puree can be stored in Sage Spoonfuls jars for up to 3 days in the refrigerator and up to 3 months in the freezer.

Serving
Asparagus puree should be served warm and tastes best when mixed with other foods. For a creamier consistency and added nutrition, mix puree with a little breast milk, formula, or stock and a baby cereal or grain (rice, barley, millet, quinoa, or amaranth). Add a pinch of fresh mint, tarragon, or grated cheese for extra flavor.

On-The-Go
Stored in Sage Spoonfuls jars, asparagus puree will stay fresh in your cooler, with the frozen ice pack, for up to 12 hours and out of the refrigerator or cooler for up to 2 hours.

All About Asparagus
Asparagus contains a surprising amount of protein for a vegetable and is a good choice for babies on a vegetarian diet. It is also a known diuretic and may give your baby's urine a strong smell. This is normal and is due to the amino acid asparagine. Look for firm asparagus stalks that are a deep green color—the deeper the color, the more nutrient-dense it will be. Asparagus should be prepared within 2–3 days of purchasing, because it is perishable and loses nutrients relatively quickly. Frozen asparagus can also be used.

Yummy Combinations With Asparagus

With Fruit

Asparagus and Apple
Asparagus and Pear

Combine purees in equal parts. They taste great both warm and cool. Try mixing yummy combo with a little breast milk or formula and a baby cereal or grain (rice, millet, quinoa, or amaranth) and serve warm. They will stay fresh in your cooler, with the frozen ice pack, for 12 hours and out or the refrigerator or cooler for 2 hours.

With Vegetables

Asparagus and Carrot
Asparagus and Potato
Asparagus and Parsnip
Asparagus and Sweet Potato
Asparagus and Cauliflower

Asparagus and Zucchini
Asparagus and Butternut Squash
Asparagus, Carrot, and Potato
Asparagus, Leek, and Potato
Asparagus, Leek, and Sweet Potato

Combine purees in equal parts. They taste best warm, but can also be served cool. Try mixing yummy combo with a little breast milk, formula, or stock and a baby cereal or grain (rice, barley, millet, quinoa, or amaranth) and serve warm. Add some grated cheese for extra flavor. These combos can also be mixed with small shaped pasta, with the exception of potato and sweet potato. They will stay fresh in your cooler, with the frozen ice pack, for 12 hours and out of the refrigerator or cooler for 2 hours.

With Meat

Asparagus and Chicken, Turkey, Lamb, or Pork
Asparagus, Potato, and Chicken, Turkey, Lamb, or Pork
Asparagus, Parsnip, and Chicken, Turkey, Lamb, or Pork
Asparagus, Carrot, and Chicken, Turkey, Lamb, or Pork
Asparagus, Sweet Potato, and Chicken, Turkey, Lamb, or Pork
Asparagus, Butternut Squash, and Chicken, Turkey, Lamb, or Pork

Combine purees in equal parts. They should be served warm. Try mixing yummy combo with a little breast milk, formula, or stock and a baby cereal or grain (rice, barley, millet, amaranth, or quinoa). Add a pinch of fresh parsley, tarragon, or grated cheese for extra flavor. These combos can also be mixed with small shaped pasta, with the exception of potato and sweet potato. They should not be out of the refrigerator for more than 1 hour.

tomato

2 Medium Tomatoes = 7 oz puree

EXCELLENT SOURCE OF:
VITAMIN C
VITAMIN A
VITAMIN K

GOOD SOURCE OF:
POTASSIUM
MANGANESE
FIBER
VITAMIN B6
FOLATE

ALSO CONTAINS:
VITAMIN E
THIAMIN
NIACIN
MAGNESIUM
PHOSPHOROUS
COPPER
PROTEIN
RIBOFLAVIN
IRON
ZINC
PANTOTHENIC ACID
CALCIUM

SUITABLE FOR
REFRIGERATOR
AND FREEZER

* Wash tomatoes thoroughly under cold running water, *peel, cut in half, de-seed and chop.
* Place in a steamer basket and steam for about 5 minutes.
* Puree into a mushy-mash using an immersion blender or food processor. Tomatoes are naturally juicy; you will not need extra liquid for thinning.
* Let cool and serve or store.
* Tomato puree can be stored in Sage Spoonfuls jars for up to 3 days in the refrigerator and up to 3 months in the freezer.
* To peel: mark an X on the bottom of each tomato and place into boiling water, let boil for 1 minute, remove from water and cool for 2 minutes, peel skin off.
* Raw tomatoes are too acidic for your baby at this stage; it is important to cook them before serving.

Serving
Tomato puree can be served warm or cool and tastes best when mixed with other foods. For a creamier consistency with added nutrition, mix puree with a little breast milk, formula, or stock and a baby cereal or grain (rice, barley, millet, quinoa, or amaranth). Add a pinch of fresh basil, parsley, oregano, or grated cheese for extra flavor. Tomatoes are, of course, very yummy with pasta—see page 214 for my *"Too Good To Be True"* tomato sauce recipe.

On-The-Go
Stored in Sage Spoonfuls jars, tomato puree will stay fresh in your cooler, with the frozen ice pack, for up to 12 hours and out of the refrigerator or cooler for up to 2 hours.

All About Tomatoes
Tomatoes are a wonderful and versatile food for your baby. They can be served as a fresh puree or as a sauce. Tomatoes are an excellent source of the antioxidant lycopene. While most foods lose some of their nutritional value when cooked, the lycopene content in tomatoes is actually enhanced during the cooking process. Avoid feeding your baby tomato puree or tomato sauce if she is teething or has acid reflux, as the acidity could worsen the symptoms.

Yummy Combinations With Tomato

With Vegetables

Tomato and Cauliflower
Tomato and Zucchini
Tomato and Parsnip
Tomato and Asparagus

Tomato and Butternut Squash
Tomato, Pea, and Parsnip
Tomato, Leek, and Potato
Tomato, Broccoli, and Cauliflower

Combine purees in equal parts. They taste great warm or cool. Try mixing yummy combo with a little stock and a baby cereal or grain (rice, barley, millet, amaranth, or quinoa) and serve warm. These combos can also be mixed with small shaped pasta. For extra flavor, add a pinch of fresh basil, parsley, oregano, or grated cheese. They will stay fresh in your cooler, with the frozen ice pack, for 12 hours and out of the refrigerator or cooler for 2 hours.

With Beans

Tomato and Lentil
Tomato and Split Pea
Tomato and Black Bean
Tomato, Leek, and Lentil
Tomato, Carrot, and Split Pea
Tomato, Avocado, and Black Bean
Tomato, Mango, and Black Bean

Combine purees in equal parts. They taste best warm but can also be served cool. Try mixing yummy combo with a little stock and a baby cereal or grain (rice, barley, millet, amaranth or quinoa) and serve warm. For extra flavor, add a pinch of fresh basil, parsley, oregano, or grated cheese. They will stay fresh in your cooler, with the frozen ice pack, for 12 hours and out of the refrigeratoror or cooler for 2 hours.

With Meat

Tomato, Lentil, and Chicken, Turkey, or Lamb
Tomato, Zucchini, and Chicken, or Turkey
Tomato, Broccoli, and Poultry, Pork, or Lamb
Tomato, Sweet Potato, and Poultry, Pork, or Lamb
Tomato, Butternut Squash, and Poultry, Pork, or Lamb

Combine purees in equal parts. They should be served warm. Try mixing yummy combo with a little stock and a baby cereal or grain (rice, millet, barley, amaranth, or quinoa). For extra flavor, add a pinch of fresh parsley, basil, or grated cheese. These combos should not be out of the refrigerator for more than 1 hour.

EXCELLENT SOURCE OF:
FIBER
FOLATE
MANGANESE
THIAMIN
PROTEIN
PHOSPHORUS
IRON
ZINC
MAGNESIUM
POTASSIUM
VITAMIN B6
COPPER
PANTOTHENIC ACID
CARBOHYDRATES

GOOD SOURCE OF:
NIACIN
RIBOFLAVIN
SELENIUM
VITAMIN C
VITAMIN K
CALCIUM

ALSO CONTAINS:
VITAMIN E
VITAMIN A
ZINC

SUITABLE FOR
REFRIGERATOR
AND FREEZER

lentils

1 Cup of Dry Lentils = 16 oz puree

* Place lentils in a strainer and wash thoroughly under cold running water.

* Bring 4 cups of purified water or stock to a boil in a medium saucepan over high heat. Add the lentils and let boil for about 2 minutes.

* Reduce heat to low, cover and simmer, stirring occasionally, for about 45 minutes, until the lentils are very tender and cooked through. Add more water or stock, if necessary, during the cooking process.

* Strain the lentils and puree into a mushy mash, using an immersion blender or food processor. Add cooking water or stock, as needed, to thin puree.

* Let cool and serve or store.

* Lentil puree can be stored in Sage Spoonfuls jars for up to 3 days in the refrigerator or up to 3 months in the freezer.

Serving
Lentil puree tastes best when served warm. Try mixing puree with a little stock and a baby cereal or grain (rice, millet, barley, amaranth, or quinoa). Add a pinch of fresh parsley or turmeric for extra flavor.

On-The-Go
Stored in Sage Spoonfuls jars, lentil puree will stay fresh in your cooler, with the frozen ice pack, for up to 12 hours and out of the refrigerator or cooler for up to 2 hours.

All About Lentils
Lentils are nutritional powerhouses for your baby. They have a mild flavor and make a great base to mix other foods with. Lentils are rich in iron and disease-fighting antioxidants. Lentil puree is a great source of non-meat protein and is a perfect choice for babies on a vegetarian diet or as a protein packed on-the-go food. You can use red, brown, or green lentils. They can be purchased in bulk and stored in an airtight container or package in a cool, dry place for up to 6 months.

Yummy Combinations With Lentils

With Vegetables

Lentil and Sweet Potato
Lentil and Butternut Squash
Lentil, Pea, and Leek
Lentil, Apple, and Carrot

Lentil, Leek, and Carrot
Lentil, Parsnip, and Pear
Lentil, Tomato, and Cauliflower
Lentil, Sweet Potato, and Broccoli

Combine purees in equal parts. They taste best when served warm. Try mixing yummy puree with a little stock and a baby cereal or grain (rice, millet, barley, amaranth, or quinoa). Add a pinch of fresh parsley, sage, or turmeric for extra flavor. These combinations will stay fresh in your cooler, with the frozen ice pack, for 12 hours and out of the refrigerator or cooler for 2 hours.

With Meat

Lentil and Chicken, Turkey, Pork, or Lamb
Lentil, Carrot, and Chicken, Turkey, Pork, or Lamb
Lentil, Leek, Carrot, and Chicken, Turkey, Pork, or Lamb
Lentil, Tomato, Leek, and Chicken, Turkey, Pork, or Lamb
Lentil, Sweet Potato, and Chicken, Turkey, Pork, or Lamb
Lentil, Butternut Squash, and Chicken, Turkey, Pork, or Lamb

Combine purees in equal parts. They should be served warm. Try mixing yummy combo with a little stock and a baby cereal or grain (rice, barley, millet, amaranth, or quinoa). Add a pinch of tumeric or fresh parsley for extra flavor. These combinations should not be out of the refrigerator for more than 1 hour.

split peas

1 Cup Dry Split Peas = 15 oz puree

* Place split peas in a strainer and wash thoroughly under cold running water.
* Bring 4 cups of purified water or stock to a boil in a medium saucepan over high heat. Put split peas into boiling water and let boil for 2 minutes.
* Reduce heat to low, cover and simmer for about 45 minutes, until split peas are very tender and cooked through.
* Strain peas and puree into a mushy mash using an immersion blender or food processor. Add cooking water or stock, as needed, to thin puree.
* Let cool and serve or store.
* Split pea puree can be stored in Sage Spoonfuls jars for up to 3 days in the refrigerator or up to 3 months in the freezer.

EXCELLENT SOURCE OF:
FIBER
MANGANESE
FOLATE
PROTEIN
THIAMIN
COPPER
PHOSPHORUS
CARBOHYDRATES
MAGNESIUM
POTASSIUM
IRON
ZINC
VITAMIN K
PANTOTHENIC ACID
RIBOFLAVIN
NIACIN

GOOD SOURCE OF:
VITAMIN B6
CALCIUM
VITAMIN A
VITAMIN C
SELENIUM

ALSO CONTAINS:
SODIUM

SUITABLE FOR
REFRIGERATOR
AND FREEZER

Serving
Split pea puree tastes best when served warm. Try mixing puree with a little stock and a baby cereal or grain (rice, barley, millet, amaranth, or quinoa).

On-The-Go
Stored in Sage Spoonfuls jars, split pea puree will stay fresh in your cooler, with the frozen ice pack, for 12 hours and out of the refrigerator or cooler for 2 hours.

All About Split Peas
Split pea puree is an excellent source of protein and a great choice for babies on a vegetarian diet. It is also a good protein source when on-the-go. Split peas are full of complex carbohydrates, which will help give your baby lots of energy. Additionally, they are rich in antioxidants. There are different varieties of split pea. Green are the most popular and widely available, but you can also use red and yellow. Split peas can be purchased in bulk. Stored in an airtight container or package, split peas will stay fresh for up to 1 year.

Yummy Combinations With Split Peas

With Fruit

Split Pea and Pear
Split Pea and Apple

Combine purees in equal parts. They taste best warm. Try mixing yummy combo with a little breast milk or formula and a baby cereal or grain (rice, millet, amaranth, or quinoa). They will stay fresh in your cooler, with the frozen ice pack, for 12 hours and out of the refrigerator or cooler for 2 hours.

With Vegetables

Split Pea and Pumpkin
Split Pea and Carrot
Split Pea and Sweet Potato
Split Pea and Butternut Squash
Split Pea, Leek, and Carrot
Split Pea, Parsnip, and Pear

Split Pea, Leek, and Potato
Split Pea, Carrot, and Potato
Split Pea, Parsnip, and Carrot
Split Pea, Parsnip, and Apple
Split Pea, Carrot, and Apple
Split Pea, Apple, and Butternut Squash

Combine purees in equal parts. They taste best served warm, but can also be served cool. Try mixing yummy combo with a little stock and a baby cereal or grain (rice, millet, barley, amaranth, or quinoa). They will stay fresh in your cooler, with the frozen ice pack, for 12 hours, out of the refrigerator or cooler for 2 hours.

With Meat

Split Pea and Chicken, Turkey, Pork, or Lamb
Split Pea, Carrot, and Chicken, Turkey, Pork, or Lamb
Split Pea, Parsnip, and Chicken, Turkey, Pork, or Lamb
Split Pea, Leek, Carrot, and Chicken, Turkey, Pork, or Lamb
Split Pea, Butternut Squash, and Chicken, Pork, Turkey, or Lamb

Combine purees in equal parts. They should be served warm. Try mixing yummy combo with a little stock and a baby cereal or grain (rice, barley, millet, amaranth, or quinoa). Add a pinch of fresh parsley, sage, or thyme for extra flavor. These combos should not be out of the refrigerator for more than 1 hour.

black beans

1 Cup Canned Black Beans = 6 oz puree

EXCELLENT SOURCE OF:
FOLATE
FIBER
THIAMIN
MANGANESE
PROTEIN
MAGNESIUM
POTASSIUM
COPPER
PHOSPHORUS
IRON
ZINC
CARBOHYDRATES

GOOD SOURCE OF:
VITAMIN B6
CALCIUM
RIBOFLAVIN
NIACIN
PANTOTHENIC ACID
VITAMIN K
SELENIUM

ALSO CONTAINS:
VITAMIN E

SUITABLE FOR
REFRIGERATOR
AND FREEZER

* Place black beans in a strainer and rinse thoroughly under cold running water. This will remove the excess sodium.
* Puree into a mushy mash using a food processor. Add purified water or stock, as needed, to thin puree.
* Black bean puree can be stored in Sage Spoonfuls jars for up to 3 days in the refrigerator and up to 3 months in the freezer.

Serving
Black Bean puree tastes great warm or cool. Try mixing puree with a little stock and a baby cereal or grain (rice, barley, millet, amaranth, or quinoa) and serve warm. Add some grated cheese for extra flavor.

On-The-Go
Stored in Sage Spoonfuls jars, black bean puree will stay fresh in your cooler, with the frozen ice pack, for up to 12 hours and out of the refrigerator or cooler for up to 2 hours.

All About Black Beans
Black beans have a smooth, soft texture and a hearty, yet sweet, taste. They are loaded with protein, antioxidants, vitamins, and minerals, making them a great choice for a baby on a vegetarian diet or as a source of protein for on-the-go. Dried black beans can be purchased in bulk and will stay fresh for up to 12 months, when stored in an airtight container in your cupboard. Using pre-cooked, canned black beans saves a lot of prep time; just be sure to rinse thoroughly before pureeing.

Yummy Combinations With Black Beans

With Fruit

Black Bean and Avocado Black Bean and Banana
Black Bean and Mango   Black Bean, Mango, and Banana

Combine purees in equal parts. They taste great warm or cool. Try mixing yummy combo with a little breast milk, formula, or stock and a baby cereal or grain (rice, barley, millet, amaranth, or quinoa) and serve warm. With the exception of avocado, these combos will stay fresh in your cooler, with the cold pack, for 12 hours and out of the refrigerator or cooler for 2 hours. Mash fresh avocado into the black beans when on-the-go to avoid discoloration.

With Vegetables

Black Bean and Carrot   Black Bean, Potato, and Carrot
Black Bean and Pumpkin   Black Bean, Tomato, and Avocado
Black Bean and Butternut Squash Black Bean, Banana, and Pumpkin
Black Bean and Sweet Potato   Black Bean, Carrot, and Leek

Combine purees together in equal parts. They taste great warm or cool. Try mixing yummy combo with a little stock and a baby cereal or grain (rice, barley, millet, amaranth, or quinoa) and serve warm. Add a pinch of fresh parsley, cilantro, or grated cheese for extra flavor. These combos will stay fresh in your cooler, with the frozen ice pack, for 12 hours and out of the refrigerator or cooler for 2 hours.

With Meat

Black Bean and Chicken or Turkey
Black Bean, Tomato, and Chicken or Turkey
Black Bean, Banana, and Chicken or Turkey
Black Bean, Mango, and Chicken or Turkey
Black Bean, Butternut Squash, and Chicken or Turkey
Black Bean, Avocado, Tomato, and Chicken or Turkey

Combine purees in equal parts. They should be served warm. Try mixing yummy combo with a little stock and a baby cereal or grain (rice, millet, barley, amaranth, or quinoa). Add a pinch of fresh cilantro, parsley, or grated cheese for extra flavor. These combos should not be out of the refrigerator for more than 1 hour.

chicken

1 lb of Ground Chicken = 16 oz puree

* Pour 1 cup of purified water or stock into a medium skillet. Bring the liquid to a boil over high heat.
* Add ground chicken and reduce heat to medium–high. Cook for about 3 minutes until chicken is cooked through and no longer pink. Use the end of a spatula to break up chicken while it cooks so the pieces stay small.
* Using a slotted spoon, transfer the chicken to a food processor.
* Puree into a mushy mash using a food processor. Add stock as needed while pureeing to achieve desired consistency. It may look a little pasty, but it tastes delicious.
* Let cool and serve or store.
* Chicken puree can be stored in Sage Spoonfuls jars for up to 3 days in the refrigerator and up to 1 month in the freezer.

EXCELLENT SOURCE OF:
NIACIN
PROTEIN
VITAMIN
VITAMIN B6
SELENIUM
PHOSPHORUS

GOOD SOURCE OF:
PANTOTHENIC ACID
MAGNESIUM
POTASSIUM
VITAMIN B12
RIBOFLAVIN
ZINC

ALSO CONTAINS:
THIAMIN
IRON
SODIUM
VITAMIN C
FOLATE
CALCIUM
COPPER
MANGANESE

Serving
Chicken puree should be served warm and is best when mixed with other food. Try mixing puree with a little breast milk, formula, or stock and a baby cereal or grain (rice, barley, millet, amaranth, or quinoa). It can also be mixed with small shaped pasta. Add a pinch of fresh parsley, sage, rosemary, yellow curry powder, or grated cheese for extra flavor.

On-The-Go
Chicken puree should not be out of the refrigerator for more than 1 hour.

All About Chicken
Chicken is a great first meat for your baby. It has a mild, pleasing flavor, is naturally lean, and is easy to digest. Dark meat contains twice the amount of iron and zinc as white meat. Whenever possible, buy organic, free range chicken, because it has not been treated with hormones, steroids, or antibiotics, and it contains DHA. Be sure to check the expiration date on the package. Raw chicken will stay fresh, wrapped properly, for up to 3 days in the refrigerator and up to 3 months in the freezer. Be sure to put chicken into the refrigerator or freezer as soon as you get home.

SUITABLE FOR
REFRIGERATOR
AND FREEZER

Yummy Combinations With Chicken

With Fruit

Chicken and Apricot	Chicken and Pear
Chicken and Peach	Chicken and Apple
Chicken and Avocado	Chicken, Banana, and Peach
Chicken and Banana	Chicken, Banana, and Mango
Chicken and Mango	Chicken, Banana, and Avocado

Combine purees in equal parts. They should be served warm. Try mixing yummy combo with a little breast milk or formula and a baby cereal or grain (rice, barley, millet, amaranth, or quinoa). These combos should not be out of the refrigerator for more than 1 hour.

With Vegetables

Chicken and Carrot	Chicken, Leek, and Potato
Chicken and Potato	Chicken, Parsnip, and Pear
Chicken and Pea	Chicken, Broccoli, and Potato
Chicken and Parsnip	Chicken, Carrot, and Asparagus
Chicken and Broccoli	Chicken, Cauliflower, and Broccoli
Chicken and Green Bean	Chicken, Sweet Potato, and Pea
Chicken and Sweet Potato	Chicken, Sweet Potato, and Apple
Chicken and Butternut Squash	Chicken, Leek, and Butternut Squash

Combine purees in equal parts. They should be served warm. Try mixing yummy combo with a little breast milk, formula, or stock and a baby cereal or grain (rice, barley, millet, amaranth, or quinoa). These combos can also be mixed with small shaped pasta, with the exception of sweet potato and potato. Add a pinch of fresh parsley, sage, rosemary, yellow curry powder, or grated cheese for extra flavor. These combos should not be out of the refrigerator for more than 1 hour.

With Beans

Chicken, Carrot, and Lentil	Chicken, Sweet Potato, and Lentil
Chicken, Leek, and Split Pea	Chicken, Tomato, and Black Bean
Chicken, Pumpkin, and Lentil	Chicken, Butternut Squash, and Lentil
Chicken, Carrot, and Split Pea	Chicken, Avocado, and Black Bean

Combine purees in equal parts. They should be served warm. Try mixing yummy combo with a little stock and a baby cereal or grain (rice, barley, millet, amaranth, or quinoa). These combos should not be out of the refrigerator for more than 1 hour.

turkey

1 lb Ground Turkey = 16 oz puree

EXCELLENT SOURCE OF:
PROTEIN
SELENIUM
NIACIN
VITAMIN B6
PHOSPHORUS

GOOD SOURCE OF:
VITAMIN B12
POTASSIUM
ZINC
MAGNESIUM
RIBOFLAVIN
PANTOTHENIC ACID
IRON
COPPER

ALSO CONTAINS:
THIAMIN
FOLATE
SODIUM
MANGANESE
CALCIUM

SUITABLE FOR
REFRIGERATOR
AND FREEZER

* Pour 1 cup of purified water or stock into a medium sized skillet and bring to a boil over high heat.
* Add ground turkey and lower heat to medium–high. Cook for about 3 minutes until cooked through and no longer pink. Continuously break up turkey with the end of a spatula, so the pieces stay small.
* With a slotted spoon, transfer cooked turkey to a food processor.
* Puree to a mushy mash with a food processor. Add cooking water or stock, as needed, to thin puree. It may have a pasty consistency, but it tastes great.
* Let cool and serve or store.
* Turkey can be stored in Sage Spoonfuls jars for up to 3 days in the refrigerator or up to 1 month in freezer.

Serving
Turkey puree should be served warm and is best when mixed with other food. Try mixing puree with a little stock and a baby cereal or grain (rice, barley, millet, amaranth, or quinoa). Add a pinch of fresh parsley or grated cheese for extra flavor. Turkey puree can also be mixed with small shaped pasta.

On-The-Go
Turkey puree should not be out of the refrigerator for more than 1 hour.

All About Turkey
Turkey is a great first meat for your baby; it is naturally lean, easy to digest, and high in protein. It also contains tryptophan, a building block of serotonin, which is a natural sleep aid. Whenever possible, buy turkey that has not been treated with hormones, steroids, or antibiotics. Be sure to check the expiration date on the package and put the turkey into the refrigerator or freezer as soon as you get home. When wrapped properly, turkey will stay fresh in the refrigerator for 3 days and up to 3 months in the freezer.

Yummy Combinations With Turkey

With Fruit

Turkey and Apple
Turkey and Pear
Turkey and Apricot

Turkey, and Banana
Turkey, and Peach
Turkey, Banana, and Mango

Combine purees in equal parts. They should be served warm. Try mixing yummy combo with a little breast milk or formula and a baby cereal or grain (rice, millet, amaranth, or quinoa). These combos should not be out of the refrigerator for more than 1 hour.

With Vegetables

Turkey and Pea
Turkey and Pumpkin
Turkey and Parsnip
Turkey and Potato
Turkey and Green Bean
Turkey and Sweet Potato
Turkey and Butternut Squash

Turkey, Zucchini, and Apple
Turkey, Carrot, and Broccoli
Turkey, Apple, and Carrot
Turkey, Parsnip, and Pea
Turkey, Carrot, and Broccoli
Turkey, Apple, and Potato
Turkey, Asparagus, and Sweet Potato

Combine purees in equal parts. They should be served warm. Try mixing yummy combo with a little stock and a baby cereal or grain (rice, barley, millet, amaranth, or quinoa). Add a pinch of of fresh thyme, basil, parsley, or grated cheese for extra flavor. With the exception of sweet potato/potato, these combos can also be mixed with small shaped pasta. They should not be out of the refrigerator for more than 1 hour.

With Beans

Turkey, Leek, and Split Pea or Lentil
Turkey, Butternut Squash, and Split Pea or Lentil
Turkey, Parsnip, and Split Pea or Lentil
Turkey, Sweet Potato, and Split Pea or Lentil
Turkey, Tomato, and Black Bean
Turkey, Mango, Avocado, and Black Bean

Combine purees in equal parts. They should be served warm. Try mixing yummy combo with a little stock and a baby cereal or grain (rice, barley, millet, amaranth, or quinoa). Add a pinch of fresh parsley or grated cheese for extra flavor. These combos should not be out of the refrigerator for more than 1 hour.

7-9 MONTHS

EXCELLENT SOURCE OF:
THIAMIN
SELENIUM
PROTEIN
VITAMIN B6
NIACIN
PHOSPHOROUS
RIBOFLAVIN
ZINC
VITAMIN B12
PANTOTHENIC ACID

GOOD SOURCE OF:
IRON
POTASSIUM
COPPER
MAGNESIUM
SODIUM
VITAMIN E
MANGANESE

ALSO CONTAINS:
CALCIUM

SUITABLE FOR
REFRIGERATOR
AND FREEZER

pork

½ lb Pork Tenderloin = 8 oz puree

⁎ Preheat oven to 425 degrees and line a baking sheet with unbleached parchment paper.

⁎ Trim the fat and silver membrane from pork, place pork on baking sheet, and brush lightly with olive oil (optional).

⁎ Place the baking sheet in the oven on the center rack and roast for 25 minutes.

⁎ Remove pork from oven and let stand for 10 minutes. Doing this allows the juices to redistribute, if you cut too soon, all the juice will run out of the meat.

⁎ Puree into a mushy mash using a food processor. Add stock while pureeing, as needed, to achieve desired consistency. The puree will be pasty, but delicious.

⁎ Let cool and serve or store.

⁎ Pork puree can be stored in Sage Spoonfuls jars for up to 3 days in the refrigerator or up to 1 month in freezer.

Serving
Pork puree should be served warm and is best mixed with other food. Try mixing puree with a little stock and a baby cereal or grain (rice, barley, millet, amaranth, or quinoa). Add a pinch of fresh parsley or grated cheese for extra flavor. It can also be mixed with small shaped pasta.

On-The-Go
Pork puree should not be out of the refrigerator for more than 1 hour.

All About Pork
Pork is a great first meat for your baby; it is naturally lean, high in protein, and has a pleasing taste. Whenever possible, buy pork that has not been treated with steroids, antibiotics, or hormones. Look for it to be a deep red color and double check the expiration date before purchasing. Make sure to keep it tightly wrapped and place in the refrigerator or freezer as soon as you get home. Pork will stay fresh in the refrigerator for up to 3 days and in the freezer for up to 3 months.

Yummy Combinations With Pork

With Fruit

Pork and Pear
Pork and Plum
Pork and Apricot
Pork and Apple
Pork and Peach

Pork and Mango
Pork, Plum, and Pear
Pork, Banana, and Apple
Pork, Banana, and Peach
Pork, Banana, and Cherry

Combine purees in equal parts. They should be served warm. Try mixing yummy combo with a little breast milk or formula and a baby cereal or grain (rice, millet, oatmeal or quinoa). These combos should not be out of the refrigerator for more than 1 hour.

With Vegetables

Pork and Pea
Pork and Parsnip
Pork and Asparagus
Pork and Green Bean
Pork and Sweet Potato/Potato
Pork and Butternut Squash
Pork, Pea, and Carrot

Pork, Pea, and Potato
Pork, Apple, and Carrot
Pork, Mango, and Tomato
Pork, Leek, and Sweet Potato
Pork, Apple, and Sweet Potato
Pork, Cauliflower, and Broccoli
Pork, Leek, and Butternut Squash

Combine purees in equal parts. They should be served warm. Try mixing yummy combo with a little stock and a baby cereal or grain (rice, millet, barley, amaranth, or quinoa). Add a pinch of fresh sage, parsley, or grated cheese for extra flavor. They can also be mixed with small shaped pasta, with the exception of potato and sweet potato. These combos should not be out of the refrigerator for more than 1 hour.

With Beans

Pork, Carrot, and Split Pea
Pork, Mango, and Black Bean
Pork, Sweet Potato, and Lentil
Pork, Butternut Squash, and Lentil
Pork, Banana, and Black Bean

Combine purees in equal parts. They should be served warm. Try mixing yummy combo with a little stock and a baby cereal or grain (rice, millet, barley, amaranth, or quinoa). Add a pinch of fresh sage or parsley for extra flavor. These combos should not be out of the refrigerator for more than 1 hour.

EXCELLENT SOURCE OF:
PROTEIN
NIACIN
VITAMIN B12
VITAMIN B6
ZINC
PHOSPHORUS
RIBOFLAVIN
SELENIUM
THIAMIN
IRON
POTASSIUM
COPPER
PANTOTHENIC ACID
MAGNESIUM

GOOD SOURCE OF:
SODIUM

ALSO CONTAINS:
CALCIUM
MANGANESE

SUITABLE FOR
REFRIGERATOR
AND FREEZER

lamb

3 Lamb Chops (1" thick) = 4 oz puree

❋ Preheat oven to 400 Degrees and line a baking sheet with unbleached parchment paper.

❋ Place lamb chops on baking sheet and brush lightly with olive oil (optional).

❋ Place baking sheet in the oven on the center rack and roast for about 20 minutes.

❋ Remove lamb from oven and let sit for 5 minutes.

❋ Cut the lamb into pieces, discarding the fat and bones.

❋ Puree into a mushy mash using a food processor. Add purified water or stock, as needed while pureeing to achieve the proper consistency. The puree may be a little pasty, but it tastes delicious.

❋ Let cool and serve or store.

❋ Lamb puree can be stored in Sage Spoonfuls jars for up to 3 days in the refrigerator or up to 1 month in the freezer.

Serving
Lamb puree should be served warm and is best when mixed with other food. Try mixing puree with a little stock and a baby cereal or grain (rice, barley, millet, amaranth, or quinoa). Add a pinch of fresh rosemary, parsley, mint, turmeric, or yellow curry powder for extra flavor.

On-The-Go
Lamb puree should not be out of the refrigerator for more than 1 hour.

All About Lamb
Lamb puree is a good first meat for your baby; it is easy to digest and has a mild, comforting taste. Lamb is rich in many nutrients including iron, protein, and Vitamin B12. Look for lamb that has firm, pink flesh with white fat. Be sure to check the expiration date before purchasing and put the lamb in the refrigerator or freezer as soon as you get home. It will stay fresh, wrapped properly, in the refrigerator for 3 days and the freezer for 3 months.

Yummy Combinations With Lamb

With Fruit

Lamb and Pear
Lamb and Plum
Lamb and Apricot
Lamb and Apple

Lamb and Prune
Lamb and Peach
Lamb, Banana, and Peach
Lamb, Apple, and Banana

Combine purees in equal parts. They should be served warm. Try mixing yummy combo with a little breast milk or formula and a baby cereal or grain (rice, millet, or quinoa). These combos should not be out of the refrigerator for more than 1 hour.

With Vegetables

Lamb and Potato
Lamb and Parsnip
Lamb and Sweet Potato
Lamb and Butternut Squash
Lamb, Carrot, and Potato

Lamb, Pea, and Potato
Lamb, Peach, and Pumpkin
Lamb, Apricot, and Cauliflower
Lamb, Leek, and Butternut Squash
Lamb, Apple, and Butternut Squash

Combine purees in equal parts. They should be served warm. Try mixing yummy combo with a little stock and a baby cereal or grain (rice, barley, millet, amaranth, or quinoa). Add a pinch of fresh parsley, yellow curry powder, or tumeric for extra flavor. These combos should not be out of the refrigerator for more than 1 hour.

With Beans

Lamb and Lentil
Lamb and Split Pea
Lamb, Carrot, and Split Pea
Lamb, Butternut Squash, and Lentil
Lamb, Leek, and Split Pea or Lentil
Lamb, Sweet Potato, and Split Pea or Lentil

Combine purees in equal parts. They should be served warm. Try mixing yummy combo with a little stock and a baby cereal or grain (rice, barley, millet, amaranth, or quinoa). Add a pinch of fresh sage, parsley, rosemary, or turmeric for extra flavor. These combos should not be out of the refrigerator for more than 1 hour.

quinoa

½ Cup Quinoa = 1 cup prepared

EXCELLENT SOURCE OF:
MANGANESE
MAGNESIUM
PHOSPHOROUS
FIBER
FOLATE
CARBOHYDRATES

GOOD SOURCE OF:
PROTEIN
IRON
THIAMIN
ZINC
RIBOFLAVIN
VITAMIN B6
POTASSIUM
SELENIUM
VITAMIN E

ALSO CONTAINS:
NIACIN
CALCIUM
SODIUM

**SUITABLE FOR
REFRIGERATOR
AND FREEZER**

* Place dry quinoa in a strainer and rinse thoroughly under cold running water.
* Bring 1 cup of water or stock to a boil in a small saucepan over high heat
* Add quinoa and boil for 1 minute; then reduce heat to low, cover, and simmer for about 20 minutes, stirring occasionally, until all the liquid has been absorbed. Add more water or stock while cooking, if necessary.
* Turn off heat and fluff quinoa with a fork.
* Let cool and serve or store.
* Cooked quinoa can be stored in Sage Spoonfuls jars for up to 3 days in the refrigerator.

Serving
Quinoa tastes great warm or cool. For a creamier consistency with added nutrition, mix quinoa with a little breast milk or formula and a fruit puree. Quinoa is also delicious when mixed with a little stock and veggies, beans, pork, lamb, poultry, and, when your baby is older, beef and fish.

On-The-Go
Stored in Sage Spoonfuls jars, prepared quinoa will stay fresh in your cooler, with the frozen ice pack, for 12 hours and out of the refrigerator or cooler for 2 hours (1 hour when mixed with meat, poultry, or fish).

All About Quinoa
Quinoa is a true superfood. It is a complete protein making it an excellent choice for vegetarian babies. It is also gluten and wheat-free, easy to digest and non-allergenic. Quinoa is considered a grain, but it is actually a seed. Yellow is the most popular and widely available variety, but it also comes in other varieties such as black, orange, and purple. Quinoa can be found in the bulk section of natural markets, specialty food stores, and online. Stored in an airtight container, quinoa will stay fresh in a cool, dry place for up to 3 months. When stored in the refrigerator, it will stay fresh for up to 6 months.

amaranth

½ Cup Amaranth = 1 cup prepared

⁎ Place dry amaranth into a strainer and rinse thoroughly under cold running water.

⁎ Bring 1 ½ cups of purified water or stock to a boil in a small saucepan over high heat.

⁎ Add amaranth and let boil for 1 minute, reduce heat to low, cover and let simmer for 20–25 minutes, stirring occasionally, until all the liquid is absorbed. Add more water or stock while cooking, if necessary.

⁎ Remove from heat and fluff with a fork.

⁎ Let cool and serve or store

⁎ Amaranth can be stored in Sage Spoonfuls jars for up to 3 days in the refrigerator or up to 3 months in the freezer.

Serving
Amaranth tastes great warm and cool. For a creamier consistency with added nutrition, mix amaranth with a little breast milk or formula and a fruit or veggie puree. Amaranth is also delicious with meat, poultry, and, when your baby is older, fish.

On-The-Go
Stored in Sage Spoonfuls jars, cooked amaranth will stay fresh in your cooler, with the frozen ice pack, for up to 12 hours and out of the refrigerator or cooler for up to 2 hours (1 hour when mixed with meat, poultry or fish).

All About Aramanth
Amaranth is an ancient seed that has recently gone mainstream. It is gluten-free and has a hearty, yet sweet flavor. Amaranth is exceptionally high in nutrients and makes a great staple in your baby's diet. It is an especially good choice for vegetarian babies, because it is rich in highly absorbable plant-based protein. Amaranth can be purchased in bulk and will stay fresh in an airtight container, stored in your pantry for up to 1 year.

7–9 MONTHS AND UP

EXCELLENT SOURCE OF:
MANGANESE
MAGNESIUM
PHOSPHORUS
IRON
SELENIUM
FIBER
PROTEIN
COPPER
ZINC
CARBOHYDRATES

GOOD SOURCE OF:
VITAMIN B6
FOLATE
CALCIUM
POTASSIUM

ALSO CONTAINS:
POTASSIUM
VITAMIN K
PANTOTHENIC ACID
CALCIUM

7-9 MONTHS

SUITABLE FOR REFRIGERATOR AND FREEZER

Notes:

10–12months

MORE PLEASE!

10–12 MONTHS

What is the proper consistency for this stage?

This is the stage where your baby will really learn how to chew. He most likely has a couple of teeth he's been chomping away with already. If he is ready, you can bump up the texture of his meals to chunk-a-licious. I consider this a thick and lumpy puree or meal. However, be sure to keep the chunks soft so as to avoid a potential choking hazard. Keep in mind that every baby is different, so play around with texture and thickness in a way your baby can handle.

At this stage, your baby may even be ready to have some of her meals finely chopped with a knife instead of being pureed. Additionally, she may also be able to tackle all grains in their whole form, barley, rice, and oatmeal included. However, if you feel your baby is not ready for this yet, please mash or lightly puree her grains before serving. You can also introduce pasta shapes that are slightly larger, like ditallini, if your baby is ready. Again, if she is not quite ready yet, please stay with small shaped pasta, like pastina or stellini.

How much solid food should my baby eat per day at this stage?

At this stage your baby will most likely be eating 3 meals per day, in addition to finger food snacks. Each meal will be around 4–6 oz. However, the size of the meals will depend on your baby, his appetite, and his pediatrician's recommendations. Be sure he is still getting the appropriate amount of breast milk or formula (roughly 18–24 oz of breast milk or formula per day at this stage).

Mealtime is becoming really messy all of a sudden, is this normal?

This is about the time your baby will start to refuse eating from a spoon. This is totally normal. She will want to explore and feed herself with her hands. It may be a mess, but is all part of the journey. While she may show interest in holding a baby spoon, it won't be until 2 years or older that she'll be able to feed herself efficiently with utensils. It'll be a while of eating with hands and making a mess! Splat mats are really great to keep under her high chair for this stage.

While this is a messy time for you, it is a fun time for your baby. The goal is not to encourage throwing food and making a mess, of course; just not to get too worried about it—your dog will love it. Our dog Charlie used to wait anxiously near Brendan at mealtime, because he knew that tasty morsels would soon be falling from the table.

Is it safe to introduce soft cheeses at this stage?

It is okay to introduce ricotta and mozzarella cheeses. However, you need to wait until your baby is at least 12 months before introducing cheeses like Blue Cheese, Goat Cheese, and Feta, because they pose a risk for listeria poisoning.

Are there any other grains that I can introduce?

Now is a great time to introduce whole grain pastas. While whole wheat should be avoided the first year, try spelt, kamut, quinoa, spinach, or brown rice pasta. They are much higher in nutrients than white pasta and make a great addition to your baby's menu.

What are the appropriate finger foods for this stage?

If your baby is ready, you can start giving her more advanced finger foods. These include:

* Steamed soybeans (edamame), cooked chickpeas, or lima beans
* Bite size pieces of roasted sweet potato, potato or eggplant
* Bite size pieces of kiwi and watermelon
* Lightly steamed blueberries, raspberries, and chopped strawberries
* Cooked pieces of pasta, such as fusilli and penne
* Lightly steamed bell pepper strips, green beans, and carrot sticks
* Toast fingers with mushy spreads like: egg yolk and avocado, blackberry and cream cheese, hummus and cucumber

Choking Hazards

Never give your baby these as finger foods at this stage:

* Hot dog pieces
* Jellybeans
* Hard raw fruit and veggies like carrots and apples (steam them first)
* Popcorn or pretzels
* Whole grapes (be sure to cut them in half; if grapes are big, quarter them)
* Cherries, raisins, or dried apricots
* Nuts or Seeds...or anything else that may pose a choking risk to your baby.

 Babies love being on the floor; be sure to wash his/her hands before giving finger food. **NEVER** leave your child unattended when he is eating.

10-12 MONTHS

strawberries

10 Medium Strawberries = 10 oz puree

EXCELLENT SOURCE OF:
VITAMIN C
MANGANESE
FIBER

GOOD SOURCE OF:
FOLATE
POTASSIUM
MAGNESIUM
VITAMIN K
PANTOTHENIC ACID

ALSO CONTAINS:
VITAMIN B6
PHOSPHOROUS
COPPER
NIACIN
IRON
VITAMIN E
PROTEIN
THIAMIN
RIBOFLAVIN
CALCIUM
ZINC
SELENIUM

SUITABLE FOR
REFRIGERATOR
AND FREEZER

* Place strawberries in a strainer and wash thoroughly under cold running water, trim off green tops and discard.
* Place strawberries in steamer basket and steam for 3 minutes (5–7 minutes if using frozen).
* Puree until chunk-a-licious using an immersion blender or food processor. If desired, remove seeds by pushing puree through a strainer, placed over a bowl, with the back of a spoon/spatula. This will give the strawberry puree a more syrupy consistency.
* Let cool and serve or store.
* Strawberry puree can be stored in Sage Spoonfuls jars for up to 3 days in the refrigerator or up to 3 months in the freezer.
* **No cook puree!** Strawberries can be pureed without steaming, if desired.

Serving
Strawberry puree can be served warm or cool and is best when mixed with other food. Try mixing puree with a little breast milk or formula and a baby cereal or grain (rice, oatmeal, amaranth, or quinoa) and serve warm. Strawberry puree can also be mixed with yogurt, silken tofu, ricotta, or cottage cheese and served cool. For extra flavor, add a pinch of cinnamon, nutmeg or ginger.

On-The-Go
Stored in Sage Spoonfuls jars, strawberry puree will stay fresh in your cooler, with the frozen ice pack, for up to 12 hours, out of the refrigerator or cooler for 2 hours (1 hour when mixed with yogurt, tofu, or cheese).

All About Strawberries
Strawberries are rich in cancer-fighting flavonoids. However, as they have some of the highest pesticide residues, buy organic whenever possible. Look for firm, plump strawberries that have a deep red color, with the green tops attached. They will not ripen any further once picked, so avoid strawberries that are yellow or look under ripe. Strawberries will stay fresh, in their container or a plastic bag, in the refrigerator for 5–7 days. You can use frozen strawberries when fresh are out of season. If you have a family history of allergies, consult your pediatrician before introducing strawberries. Strawberries stain—take care when preparing and serving.

Yummy Combinations With Strawberries

With Fruit

Strawberry and Pear
Strawberry and Peach
Strawberry and Mango
Strawberry and Apple
Strawberry and Pineapple
Strawberry and Banana
Strawberry and Kiwi
Strawberry and Blueberry
Strawberry and Cantaloupe
Strawberry, Kiwi, and Pineapple

Strawberry, Plum, and Banana
Strawberry, Kiwi, and Banana
Strawberry, Peach, and Banana
Strawberry, Peach, and Blueberry
Strawberry, Blueberry, and Banana
Strawberry, Raspberry, and Banana
Strawberry, Raspberry, and Peach
Strawberry, Blackberry, and Banana
Strawberry, Banana, and Pineapple
Strawberry, Banana, and Cantaloupe

Combine purees in equal parts. They taste great warm or cool. Try mixing yummy combo with a little breast milk or formula and a baby cereal or grain (rice, oatmeal, amaranth, or quinoa) and serve warm. They can also be mixed with yogurt, silken tofu, ricotta, or cottage cheese and served cool. For extra flavor, add a pinch of cinnamon, nutmeg, or ginger. These combos will stay fresh in your cooler, with the frozen ice pack, for 12 hours and out of the refrigerator or cooler for 2 hours (1 hour when mixed with yogurt, cheese, or tofu).

kiwi

2 Kiwi = 4 oz puree

* Peel kiwi and cut into cubes.
* Place in steamer basket and steam for about 3 minutes.
* Mash until chunk-a-licious with the back of a fork, an immersion blender or food processor.
* Let cool and serve or store.
* Kiwi puree can be stored in Sage Spoonfuls jars for up to 3 days in the refrigerator or up to 3 months in the freezer.
* **No cook puree!** Kiwis can be pureed without steaming, if desired.

Serving
Kiwi puree is a little too tart on its own and is best when mixed with other food. Try mixing puree with yogurt, silken tofu, ricotta, or cottage cheese.

On-The-Go
Stored in Sage Spoonfuls jars, kiwi puree will stay fresh in your cooler, with the frozen ice pack, for up to 12 hours and out of the refrigerator or cooler for up to 2 hours (1 hour out of refrigerator or cooler when mixed with yogurt, tofu, or cheese).

All About Kiwis
Kiwi is rich in nutrients and disease-fighting antioxidants. It is especially high in Vitamin C, which helps to promote a healthy respiratory system. Bite-sized pieces of kiwi make a great finger food for this stage. Look for kiwi that are firm, but give a little when squeezed. Let under ripe kiwi ripen on your counter. They will stay fresh at room temperature or in the refrigerator for about 5 days.

EXCELLENT SOURCE OF:
VITAMIN C
VITAMIN K
FIBER
POTASSIUM

GOOD SOURCE OF:
VITAMIN E
COPPER
FOLATE
MANGANESE
MAGNESIUM
PHOSPHORUS
CALCIUM
VITAMIN B6

ALSO CONTAINS:
PROTEIN
VITAMIN A
THIAMIN
RIBOFLAVIN
NIACIN
PANTOTHENIC ACID
IRON
ZINC
SELENIUM

SUITABLE FOR
REFRIGERATOR
AND FREEZER

Yummy Combinations With Kiwi

With Fruit

Kiwi and Pear
Kiwi and Blueberry
Kiwi and Strawberry
Kiwi and Banana
Kiwi and Cantaloupe
Kiwi, Pear, and Raspberry
Kiwi, Raspberry, and Banana

Kiwi, Banana, and Peach
Kiwi, Banana, and Strawberry
Kiwi, Banana, and Mango
Kiwi, Pineapple, and Banana
Kiwi, Blackberry, and Banana
Kiwi, Cantaloupe, and Raspberry
Kiwi, Cantaloupe, and Strawberry

Combine purees in equal parts. They taste best cool. Try mixing yummy combo with yogurt, silken tofu, ricotta, or cottage cheese. These combos will stay fresh in your cooler, with the frozen ice pack, for 12 hours and out of the refrigerator or cooler for 2 hours (1 hour when mixed with yogurt, cheese, or tofu).

10-12 MONTHS

raspberries

1 Cup of Raspberries = 4 oz puree

10–12 MONTHS AND UP

EXCELLENT SOURCE OF:
VITAMIN C
MANGANESE
FIBER
VITAMIN K

GOOD SOURCE OF:
MAGNESIUM
FOLATE
COPPER
VITAMIN E
IRON
POTASSIUM

ALSO CONTAINS:
NIACIN
PANTOTHENIC ACID
PHOSPHOROUS
THIAMIN
RIBOFLAVIN
VITAMIN B6
CALCIUM
ZINC
PROTEIN
VITAMIN A

SUITABLE FOR
REFRIGERATOR
AND FREEZER

* Put raspberries in a strainer and wash thoroughly under cold running water.
* Put in a steamer basket and steam for 3 minutes (5–7 if using frozen).
* Puree until chunk-a-licious with an immersion blender, food processor, or the back of a fork. If desired, remove seeds by pushing puree through a strainer, placed over a bowl, with the back of a spoon/spatula. This will give the puree a more syrupy consistency.
* Let cool and serve or store.
* Raspberry puree can be stored in Sage Spoonfuls jars for up to 3 days in the refrigerator or up to 3 months in the freezer.
* **No cook puree!** Raspberries can be pureed without steaming, if desired.

Serving
Raspberry puree can be served warm or cool and is best when mixed with other food. Try mixing puree with a little breast milk or formula and a baby cereal or grain (rice, oatmeal, amaranth, or quinoa) and serve warm. It can also be mixed with yogurt, silken tofu, ricotta, or cottage cheese and served cool. For extra flavor, add a pinch of cinnamon, nutmeg, or ginger.

On-The-Go
Stored in Sage Spoonfuls jars, raspberry puree will stay fresh in your cooler, with the frozen ice pack, for up to 12 hours and out of the refrigerator or cooler for up to 2 hours (1 hour out of refrigerator or cooler when mixed with yogurt, tofu, or cheese).

All About Rasberries
Raspberries are rich in nutrients and disease fighting antioxidants. Ripe raspberries have a deliciously sweet flavor that makes a great finger food for this stage. Look for raspberries that are firm, plump and have a deep red/pink color. Avoid any packages with crushed berries, because they will spoil quickly. Raspberries will stay fresh in their package or a plastic bag for about 3–5 days, in the refrigerator. Frozen raspberries are great to use when fresh are out of season. If a berry allergy runs in your family, check with your baby's pediatrician before introducing raspberries. Raspberries stain—take care when preparing and serving.

Yummy Combinations With Raspberries

With Fruit

Raspberry and Pear
Raspberry and Peach
Raspberry and Apricot
Raspberry and Kiwi
Raspberry and Plum
Raspberry and Mango
Raspberry and Banana
Raspberry and Apple
Raspberry and Pineapple
Raspberry and Cantaloupe

Raspberry, Pear, and Peach
Raspberry, Pear, and Banana
Raspberry, Cherry, and Banana
Raspberry, Kiwi, and Banana
Raspberry, Peach, and Banana
Raspberry, Mango, and Banana
Raspberry, Apricot, and Banana
Raspberry, Blueberry, and Banana
Raspberry, Cantaloupe, and Blueberry
Raspberry, Strawberry, and Blueberry

Combine purees in equal parts. They taste great warm or cool. Try mixing yummy combo with a little breast milk or formula and a baby cereal or grain (rice, oatmeal, amaranth, or quinoa) and serve warm. They can also be mixed with yogurt, silken tofu, ricotta, or cottage cheese and served cool. For extra flavor, add a pinch of cinnamon, nutmeg, or ginger. These combos will stay fresh in your cooler, with the frozen ice pack, for 12 hours and out of the refrigerator or cooler for 2 hours (1 hour when mixed with yogurt, cheese, or tofu).

With Meat

Raspberry, Mango, and Chicken, Turkey, or Pork
Raspberry, Peach, and Chicken, Turkey, or Pork
Raspberry, Banana, and Chicken, Turkey, or Pork

Combine purees in equal parts. They should be served warm. Try mixing yummy combo with a little breast milk or formula and a baby cereal or grain (rice, oatmeal, millet, amaranth, or quinoa). These combos should not be out of the refrigerator for more than 1 hour.

pineapple

¼ Pineapple = 11 oz puree

EXCELLENT SOURCE OF:
VITAMIN C
MANGANESE

GOOD SOURCE OF:
FIBER
THIAMIN
VITAMIN B6
COPPER
FOLATE
POTASSIUM
MAGNESIUM

ALSO CONTAINS:
NIACIN
PANTOTHENIC ACID
RIBOFLAVIN
IRON
PROTEIN
VITAMIN A
CALCIUM
VITAMIN K
PHOSPHOROUS
ZINC

SUITABLE FOR
REFRIGERATOR
AND FREEZER

* Wash pineapple thoroughly under cold running water, pat dry with a paper towel. Lay pineapple on its side, cut off the green top and rough bottom and discard.

* Cut pineapple in half lengthwise; then cut each piece in half lengthwise again so the pineapple is in 4 pieces. Leave ¼ of the pineapple out and store the rest in the refrigerator, in an airtight container.

* Trim off the rough core and discard. Slice the fruit away from rind. Discard rind and chop the pineapple into chunks.

* Place pineapple in steamer basket and steam for about 3 minutes (5–7 if using frozen).

* Puree until chunk-a-licious using a food processor or finely chop with a knife. Pineapples are naturally very juicy; you won't need additional liquid for thinning.

* Let cool and serve or store.

* Pineapple puree can be stored in Sage Spoonfuls jars for up to 3 days in the refrigerator or up to 3 months in the freezer.

* **No cook puree!** Pineapple can be pureed without steaming, if desired.

Serving
Pineapple puree can be served warm or cool and is best mixed with other food. Try mixing puree with breast milk or formula and a baby cereal or grain (rice, oatmeal, amaranth, or quinoa) and serve warm. It can also be mixed with yogurt, silken tofu, ricotta, or cottage cheese and served cool.

On-The-Go
Stored in Sage Spoonfuls jars, pineapple puree will stay fresh in your cooler, with the frozen ice pack, for up to 12 hours and out of the refrigerator or cooler for up to 2 hours (1 hour out of refrigerator or cooler when mixed with yogurt, tofu, or cheese).

All About Pineapple
Pineapples have a deliciously sweet and juicy tropical flavor that combines well with many different foods. Pineapple puree contains enzymes that have anti-inflammatory properties. These enzymes can also help break up mucus when your baby has a cold. Avoid giving your baby pineapple if she is teething, the acid may sting her gums. Look for pineapples that are heavy for their size and that have a sweet, fruity aroma through the skin. Ripe pineapples will stay fresh at room temperature for about 3–5 days. Frozen pineapple is great to use if fresh is unavailable.

Yummy Combinations With Pineapple

With Fruit

Pineapple and Banana
Pineapple and Mango
Pineapple and Blueberry
Pineapple and Strawberry

Pineapple, Mango, and Kiwi
Pineapple, Banana, and Strawberry
Pineapple, Raspberry, and Banana
Pineapple, Strawberry, and Blueberry

Combine purees in equal parts. They taste great warm or cool. Try mixing yummy combo with a little breast milk or formula and a baby cereal or grain (rice, oatmeal, amaranth, or quinoa) and serve warm. They can also be mixed with yogurt, silken tofu, ricotta, or cottage cheese. These combos will stay fresh in your cooler, with the frozen ice pack, for 12 hours or out of the refrigerator or cooler for 2 hours (1 hour when mixed with yogurt, tofu, or cheese).

With Vegetables And Beans

Pineapple and Sweet Potato
Pineapple and Butternut Squash
Pineapple, Banana, and Sweet Potato
Pineapple, Black Bean, and Tomato
Pineapple, Banana, and Butternut Squash

Combine purees in equal parts. They taste great warm and cool. Try mixing yummy combo with a little breast milk or formula and a baby cereal or grain (rice, millet, amaranth, or quinoa) and serve warm. These combos will stay fresh in your cooler, with the frozen ice pack, for 12 hours and out of the refrigerator or cooler for 2 hours.

With Meat

Pineapple, Mango, and Chicken, Pork, or Turkey
Pineapple, Butternut Squash, and Chicken, Pork, or Turkey
Pineapple, Banana, and Chicken, Pork, or Turkey

Combine purees in equal parts. They should be served warm. Try mixing yummy combo with a little breast milk, formula, or stock and a baby cereal or grain (rice, barley, millet, amaranth, or quinoa). These combos should not be out of the refrigerator for more than 1 hour.

blackberries

2 Cups of Blackberries = 6 oz puree

EXCELLENT SOURCE OF:
VITAMIN C
MANGANESE
VITAMIN K
FIBER

GOOD SOURCE OF:
COPPER
FOLATE
VITAMIN E
POTASSIUM
MAGNESIUM
VITAMIN A
NIACIN
IRON
ZINC

ALSO CONTAINS:
PROTEIN
PANTOTHENIC ACID
CALCIUM
PHOSPHOROUS
THIAMIN
RIBOFLAVIN
VITAMIN B6
SELENIUM

SUITABLE FOR
REFRIGERATOR
AND FREEZER

* Place blackberries in a strainer and wash thoroughly under cold running water.
* Put blackberries in steamer basket and steam for about 3 minutes (5–7 if using frozen).
* Puree until chunk-a-licious, using an immersion blender or food processor. If desired, remove the seeds by pushing the puree through a strainer, placed over a bowl, with a spoon/spatula. This will give the puree a syrupy consistency.
* Let cool and serve or store.
* Blackberry puree can be stored in Sage Spoonfuls jars for up to 3 days in the refrigerator or up to 3 months in the freezer.
* **No cook puree!** Blackberries can be pureed without steaming, if desired.

Serving
Blackberry puree can be served warm or cool and is best when mixed with other food. Try mixing puree with a little breast milk or formula and a baby cereal or grain (rice, oatmeal, amaranth, or quinoa) and serve warm. It can also be mixed with yogurt, silken tofu, ricotta, or cottage cheese and served cool. For extra flavor, add a pinch of cinnamon, nutmeg, or ginger.

On-The-Go
Stored in Sage Spoonfuls jars, blackberry puree will stay fresh in your cooler, with the frozen ice pack, for up to 12 hours and out of the refrigerator or cooler for up to 2 hours (1 hour out of refrigerator or cooler when mixed with yogurt, tofu or cheese).

All About Blackberries
Blackberries are high in disease-fighting antioxidants. Berries have some of the highest levels of pesticide residue, buy organic whenever possible. Look for blackberries that are firm, plump, and a deep purple color. Avoid any packages with crushed berries, because they will spoil quickly. Blackberries will stay fresh in their package or a plastic bag for about 3–5 days, in the refrigerator. Frozen blackberries are great to use when fresh are out of season. If you have a family history of berry allergies, consult your baby's pediatrician before serving blackberries. Blackberries stain—take care when preparing and serving.

Yummy Combinations With Blackberries

With Fruit

Blackberry and Peach
Blackberry and Pear
Blackberry and Banana
Blackberry and Kiwi
Blackberry and Mango
Blackberry and Pineapple
Blackberry and Cantaloupe
Blackberry, Apricot, and Pear

Blackberry, Banana, and Peach
Blackberry, Banana, and Mango
Blackberry, Peach, and Blueberry
Blackberry, Raspberry, and Pear
Blackberry, Strawberry, and Banana
Blackberry, Banana, and Blueberry
Blackberry, Banana, and Pineapple
Blackberry, Blueberry, and Strawberry

Combine purees in equal parts. They taste great warm or cool. Try mixing yummy combo with a little breast milk or formula and a baby cereal or grain (rice, oatmeal, amaranth, or quinoa) and serve warm. These combos can also be mixed with yogurt, silken tofu, ricotta, or cottage cheese and served cool. They will stay fresh in your cooler, with the frozen ice pack, for 12 hours or out of the refrigerator or cooler for 2 hours (1 hour when mixed with yogurt, cheese, or tofu).

With Meat

Blackberry and Pork, Chicken, Lamb, or Turkey
Blackberry, Banana, and Pork, Chicken, Lamb, or Turkey
Blackberry, Mango, and Pork, Chicken, Lamb, or Turkey
Blackberry, Apricot, and Pork, Chicken, Lamb, or Turkey

Combine purees in equal parts. They should be served warm. Try mixing yummy combo with a little breast milk, formula, or stock, and a baby cereal or grain (rice, millet, amaranth, or quinoa). These combos should not be out of the refrigerator for more than 1 hour.

corn

1 Cup of Frozen Corn = 4 oz puree

* Place corn into steamer basket and steam for 5–7 minutes.
* Puree until chunk-a-licious using an immersion blender or food processor. Add cooking water, breast milk, or formula, as needed, to thin puree.
* Let cool and serve or store.
* Corn puree can be stored in Sage Spoonfuls jars for up to 3 days in the refrigerator or up to 3 months in the freezer.

EXCELLENT SOURCE OF:
THIAMIN
FOLATE
FIBER
VITAMIN C

GOOD SOURCE OF:
CARBOHYDRATES
MAGNESIUM
PHOSPHORUS
NIACIN
PANTOTHENIC ACID
POTASSIUM
MANGANESE
PROTEIN
VITAMIN A
RIBOFLAVIN
ZINC

ALSO CONTAINS:
VITAMIN B6
IRON
COPPER
VITAMIN E
VITAMIN K
SODIUM
SELENIUM

Serving
Corn puree can be served warm or cool and is best when combined with other food. Try mixing puree with a little breast milk, formula or stock and a baby cereal or grain (rice, barley, millet, amaranth, or quinoa) and serve warm. Corn puree can also be mixed with small shaped pasta. Add a pinch of fresh parsley or grated cheese for extra flavor.

On-The-Go
Stored in Sage Spoonfuls jars, corn puree will stay fresh in your cooler, with the frozen ice pack, for up to 12 hours and out of the refrigerator or cooler for up to 2 hours.

All About Corn
Often mistaken as a vegetable, corn is actually a grain. Yellow corn is rich in lutein, which is good for your baby's eyes. Corn is one of the largest genetically modified foods; buy organic whenever possible. I like using frozen corn instead of corn on the cob; it saves a lot of prep and cooking time. If a corn allergy runs in your family, consult your child's pediatrician before introducing.

SUITABLE FOR
REFRIGERATOR
AND FREEZER

Yummy Combinations With Corn

With Fruit

Corn and Apple
Corn and Avocado

Combine purees in equal parts. They taste great warm or cool. Try mixing yummy combo with a little breast milk or formula and a baby cereal or grain (rice, oatmeal, amaranth, or quinoa) and serve warm. These combos will stay fresh in your cooler, with the frozen ice pack, for 12 hours and out of the refrigerator or cooler for 2 hours.

With Vegetables And Beans

Corn and Pea
Corn and Carrot
Corn and Beet
Corn and Green Bean
Corn and Lima Bean
Corn and Black Bean
Corn and Butternut Squash
Corn, Parsnip, and Broccoli

Corn, Tomato, and Avocado
Corn, Lima Bean, and Leek
Corn, Tomato, and Chickpea
Corn, Sweet Potato, and Apple
Corn, Zucchini, and Black Bean
Corn, Avocado, and Black Bean
Corn, Asparagus, and Bell Pepper
Corn, Butternut Squash, and Lentil

Combine purees in equal parts. They taste best warm. Try mixing yummy combo with a little breast milk, formula, or stock and a baby cereal or grain (rice, barley, millet, amaranth, or quinoa). These combos can also be mixed with pasta, with the exception of apple and avocado. Add a pinch of fresh parsley or grated cheese for extra flavor. These combos will stay fresh in your cooler, with the frozen ice pack, for 12 hours and out of the refrigerator or cooler for 2 hours.

With Meat

Corn, Sweet Potato, Leek, and Poultry, Pork, Lamb, or Beef
Corn, Carrot, and Poultry, Pork, Lamb, or Beef
Corn, Parsnip, and Poultry, Pork, Lamb, or Beef
Corn, Pea, and Poultry, Pork, Lamb, or Beef
Corn, Butternut Squash, and Poultry or Pork

Combine purees in equal parts. They should be served warm. Try mixing yummy combo with a little stock and a baby cereal or grain (rice, millet, barley, amaranth or quinoa). These combos should not be out of the refrigerator for more than 1 hour.

beets

2 Medium Beets = 6 oz puree

10–12 MONTHS AND UP

EXCELLENT SOURCE OF:
FOLATE
MANGANESE
FIBER
POTASSIUM

GOOD SOURCE OF:
VITAMIN C
MAGNESIUM
IRON
VITAMIN B6
PHOSPHOROUS
COPPER

ALSO CONTAINS:
PROTEIN
SODIUM
THIAMIN
RIBOFLAVIN
ZINC
NIACIN
PANTOTHENIC ACID
CALCIUM
SELENIUM

SUITABLE FOR
REFRIGERATOR
AND FREEZER

* Cut off beet greens and discard. Wash beets thoroughly under cold running water, peel and chop.
* Place beets in steamer basket and steam for 12–15 minutes until tender.
* Puree until chunk-a-licious, using a food processor, or finely chop with a knife. Add a little purified water, stock, breast milk or formula, if needed, to thin puree.
* Let cool and serve or store.
* Beet puree can be stored in Sage Spoonfuls jars for up to 3 days in the refrigerator or up to 3 months in the freezer.

Serving
Beet puree can be served warm or cool and is best mixed with other foods. Try mixing puree with a little breast milk, formula, or stock and a baby cereal or grain (rice, barley, millet, amaranth, or quinoa) and serve warm. It can also be mixed with yogurt, silken tofu, ricotta, or cottage cheese and served cool.

On-The-Go
Stored in Sage Spoonfuls jars, beet puree will stay fresh in your cooler, with the frozen ice pack, for up to 12 hours and out of the refrigerator or cooler for up to 2 hours.

All About Beets
Beets have a surprisingly sweet flavor. They are full of disease-fighting antioxidants and also help promote healthy liver function. Conventionally grown beets have higher nitrate levels; buy organic whenever possible. You may notice a little red color in your baby's diaper after eating beets. This is totally normal and nothing to worry about. Look for beets that are firm, have a deep purple color, and fresh greens. Whole beets will stay fresh in your refrigerator for about 2 weeks. Beets stain—take care when preparing and serving.

Yummy Combinations With Beets

With Fruit

Beet and Apple   Beet and Banana
Beet and Pear   Beet and Avocado

Combine purees in equal parts. They taste great warm or cool. Try mixing yummy combo with a little breast milk or formula and a baby cereal or grain (rice, oatmeal, amaranth or quinoa) and serve warm. These combos can also be mixed with yogurt, silken tofu, ricotta, or cottage cheese and served cool. These combos will stay fresh in your cooler, with the frozen ice pack, for 12 hours or out of the refrigerator or cooler for 2 hours (1 hour when mixed with yogurt or cheese).

With Vegetables

Beet and Carrot   Beet and Corn
Beet and Pumpkin   Beet and Broccoli
Beet and Potato   Beet and Parsnip
Beet and Chickpea   Beet and Cauliflower
Beet and Sweet Potato   Beet, Carrot, and Parsnip
Beet and Green Bean   Beet, Apple, and Carrot
Beet and Butternut Squash   Beet, Spinach, and Potato

Combine purees in equal parts. They taste best warm, but can also be served cool. Try mixing yummy combo with a little breast milk, formula, or stock and a baby cereal or grain (rice, barley, millet, amaranth, or quinoa). These combos will stay fresh in your cooler, with the frozen ice pack, for 12 hours or out of the refrigerator or cooler for 2 hours.

With Meat

Beet and Poultry, Pork, Lamb, or Beef
Beet, Spinach, Potato, and Lamb or Beef
Beet, Parsnip, and Poultry, Pork, Lamb, or Beef
Beet, Asparagus, and Poultry, Pork, Lamb, or Beef
Beet, Butternut Squash, and Poultry, Pork, Lamb, or Beef

Combine purees in equal parts. They should be served warm. Try mixing yummy combo with a little stock and a baby cereal or grain (rice, barley, millet, amaranth, or quinoa). Add a pinch of fresh parsley for extra flavor. These combos should not be out of the refrigerator for more than 1 hour.

eggplant

1 Large Eggplant = 8 oz puree

GOOD SOURCE OF:
FIBER
MANGANESE
FOLATE
POTASSIUM

ALSO CONTAINS:
VITAMIN K
VITAMIN C
NIACIN
VITAMIN B6
MAGNESIUM
COPPER
PROTEIN
THIAMIN
RIBOFLAVIN
PANTOTHENIC ACID
PHOSPHORUS
VITAMIN E
CALCIUM
IRON
ZINC

SUITABLE FOR
REFRIGERATOR
AND FREEZER

* Preheat oven to 450 and line a baking sheet with unbleached parchment paper.
* Wash eggplant thoroughly under cold running water, dry with a paper towel, slice off rough ends and discard.
* Slice eggplant in half lengthwise and place, cut side down, onto baking sheet.
* Place baking sheet in oven on center rack and roast for 20 minutes.
* Turn eggplant over and lightly brush with olive oil. Roast for 5–10 minutes more.
* Remove and discard seeds; then scoop out the flesh and puree until chunk-a-licious, using an immersion blender, food processor, or the back of a fork.
* Let cool and serve or store.
* Eggplant puree can be stored in Sage Spoonfuls jars for up to 3 days in the refrigerator or up to 3 months in the freezer.

Serving
Eggplant puree can be served warm or cool. Try mixing puree with a little breast milk, formula, or stock and a baby cereal or grain (rice, barley, millet, amaranth, or quinoa). It can also be mixed with small shaped pasta. Add a pinch of fresh basil, parsley, ginger, cinnamon or grated cheese for extra flavor.

On-The-Go
Stored in Sage Spoonfuls jars, eggplant puree will stay fresh in your cooler, with the frozen ice pack, for up to 12 hours and out of the refrigerator or cooler for up to 2 hours.

All About Eggplant
There are many different varieties of eggplant, with the Japanese purple eggplant being the most popular and widely available. Eggplant puree has a mild flavor and blends well with many different foods. Bite sized pieces of roasted eggplant make a great finger food. Look for eggplants that are heavy for their size, give a little when squeezed, and are deep purple in color, with glossy unblemished skin. Whole eggplants will stay fresh in the refrigerator for about 5 days.

Yummy Combinations With Eggplant

With Vegetables

Eggplant and Parsnip
Eggplant and Zucchini
Eggplant and Carrot
Eggplant and Sweet Potato

Eggplant and Butternut Squash
Eggplant, Corn, and Tomato
Eggplant, Spinach, and Mushroom
Eggplant, Zucchini, and Bell Pepper

Combine purees in equal parts. They taste best warm, but can also be served cool. Try mixing yummy combo with a little breast milk, formula, or stock and baby cereal or grain (rice, millet, barley, amaranth, or quinoa). They can also be mixed with small shaped pasta. For extra flavor, add a pinch of of fresh parsley, thyme, oregano, yellow curry powder, or grated cheese. These combos will stay fresh in your cooler, with the frozen ice pack, for 12 hours and out of the refrigerator or cooler for 2 hours.

With Beans

Eggplant and Lentil
Eggplant, Tomato, and Lentil
Eggplant, Carrot, and Split Pea
Eggplant, Butternut Squash, and Lentil
Eggplant, Corn, and Lima Bean
Eggplant, Tomato, Zucchini, and Chickpea

Combine purees in equal parts. They taste best warm but can also be served cool. Try mixing yummy combo with a little breast milk, formula or stock and a baby cereal or grain (rice, millet, barley, amaranth or quinoa). Add a pinch of fresh parsley, thyme, or sage for extra flavor. These combos will stay fresh in your cooler, with the frozen ice pack, for 12 hours and out of the refrigerator or cooler for 2 hours.

With Meat

Eggplant, Butternut Squash, and Lamb or Beef
Eggplant, Mushroom, and Pork, Chicken, or Turkey
Eggplant, Tomato, Pea, and Beef or Lamb
Eggplant, Spinach, Potato, and Lamb or Beef

Combine purees in equal parts. They should be served warm. Try mixing yummy combo with a little stock and a baby cereal or grain (rice, barley, millet, amaranth, or quinoa). Add a pinch of fresh parsley, turmeric, or grated cheese for extra flavor. These combos can also be mixed with small shaped pasta, with the exception of potato. They should not be out of the refrigerator for more than 1 hour.

soybeans

2 Cups Frozen Soybeans = 6 oz puree

☀

EXCELLENT SOURCE OF:
VITAMIN C
FOLATE
THIAMIN
MANGANESE
PROTEIN
CALCIUM
IRON
PHOSPHORUS
POTASSIUM
FIBER
MAGNESIUM
RIBOFLAVIN
NIACIN
ZINC
COPPER

GOOD SOURCE OF:
CARBOHYDRATES
VITAMIN A
VITAMIN B6
SELENIUM

ALSO CONTAINS:
PANTOTHENIC ACID
SODIUM

❄

SUITABLE FOR
REFRIGERATOR
AND FREEZER

✳ Place soybeans in steamer basket and steam for about 7 minutes, until tender.

✳ Puree until chunk-a-licious using a food processor or the back of a fork. Add cooking water, breast milk, formula, or stock, if needed, to thin puree.

✳ Let cool and serve or store.

✳ Soybean puree can be stored in Sage Spoonfuls jars for up to 3 days in the refrigerator or up to 3 months in the freezer.

Serving
Soybean puree can be served warm or cool. Try mixing puree with a little breast milk, formula, or stock and a baby cereal or grain (rice, barley, millet, amaranth, or quinoa) and serve warm. It can also be mixed with yogurt, silken tofu, ricotta, or cottage cheese and served cool.

On-The-Go
Stored in Sage Spoonfuls jars, soybean puree will stay fresh in your cooler, with the frozen ice pack, for up to 12 hours and out of the refrigerator or cooler for up to 2 hours (1 hour when mixed with yogurt, tofu or cheese).

All About Soybeans
Soybeans are a true superfood. They are packed with vitamins, minerals, essential fatty acids, and anti-cancer compounds. Soybeans are also rich in non-meat protein, making them an excellent food for vegetarian babies. Also called edamame, cooked soybeans make a great finger food. Soybeans are one of the largest genetically modified crops—buy organic whenever possible. Fresh soybeans should have bright green, firm shells. They are perishable and will only stay fresh in your refrigerator for about 3 days. Frozen soybeans save prep time and will stay fresh for up to 3 months in the freezer.

Yummy Combinations With Soybeans

With Fruit

Soybean and Banana
Soybean and Mango

Soybean and Peach
Soybean and Apricot

Combine purees in equal parts. They taste great warm or cool. Try mixing yummy combo with a little breast milk or formula and a baby cereal or grain (rice, oatmeal, amaranth, or quinoa) and serve warm. They can also be mixed with yogurt or cottage cheese and served cool. These combos will stay fresh in your cooler, with the frozen ice pack, for 12 hours and out of the refrigerator or cooler for 2 hours (1 hour when mixed with yogurt or cottage cheese).

With Vegetables

Soybean and Potato
Soybean and Corn
Soybean and Beet
Soybean and Carrot
Soybean and Sweet Potato

Soybean and Parsnip
Soybean and Bell Pepper
Soybean and Butternut Squash
Soybean, Corn, and Tomato

Combine purees in equal parts. They taste best warm, but can also be served cool. Try mixing yummy combo with a little breast milk, formula, or stock and a baby cereal or grain (rice, millet, barley, amaranth, or quinoa). With the exception of potato and sweet potato, these combos can be mixed with small shaped pasta. For extra flavor, add a pinch of fresh parsley or grated cheese. These combos will stay fresh in your cooler, with the frozen ice pack, for 12 hours and out of the refrigerator or cooler for 2 hours.

With Meat

Soybean, Apricot, and Lamb
Soybean, Eggplant, Tomato, and Lamb or Beef
Soybean, Parsnip, and Poultry, Pork, Lamb, or Beef
Soybean, Carrot, and Poultry, Pork, Lamb, or Beef
Soybean, Sweet Potato, and Poultry, Pork, Lamb, or Beef

Combine purees in equal parts. They should be served warm. Try mixing yummy combo with a little breast milk, formula, or stock and a baby cereal or grain (rice, millet, barley, amaranth, or quinoa). These combos should not be out of the refrigerator for more than 1 hour.

chickpeas

2 Cups Canned Chickpeas = 8 oz puree

※

EXCELLENT SOURCE OF:
FOLATE
MAGNANESE
FIBER
COPPER
PROTEIN
PHOSPHORUS
IRON
THIAMIN
MAGNESIUM
VITAMIN B6
POTASSIUM
ZINC
PANTOTHENIC ACID
RIBOFLAVIN
VITAMIN K
SELENIUM
CALCIUM
NIACIN

GOOD SOURCE OF:
VITAMIN C
VITAMIN E

ALSO CONTAINS:
VITAMIN A
SODIUM

❄

SUITABLE FOR
REFRIGERATOR
AND FREEZER

* Place chickpeas in a strainer and rinse thoroughly under cold running water to remove excess sodium.
* Puree until chunk-a-licious using a food processor. Add purified water or stock, as needed, to thin puree.
* Serve and store.
* Chickpea puree can be stored in Sage Spoonfuls jars for up to 3 days in the refrigerator or up to 3 months in the freezer.

Serving
Chickpea puree tastes great warm or cool. Try mixing puree with a little breast milk, formula or stock and a baby cereal or grain (rice, barley, millet, amaranth, or quinoa) and serve warm. Chickpea puree can also be mixed with yogurt or cottage cheese and served cool.

On-The-Go
Stored in Sage Spoonfuls jars, chickpea puree will stay fresh in your cooler, with the frozen ice pack, for up to 12 hours and out of the refrigerator or cooler for up to 2 hours (1 hour when mixed with yogurt or cottage cheese).

All About Chickpeas
Also known as garbanzo beans, chickpeas are extremely nutrient-rich and are a fantastic source of non-meat protein. They have a mild nutty taste and a velvety texture when pureed. Cooked chickpeas make a great finger food for this stage. They can be purchased dry in bulk and will stay fresh for up to one year when stored in an airtight container in a cool, dry place. I like using pre-cooked chickpeas, because it saves a lot of prep time; just make sure to rinse them before use.

Yummy Combinations With Chickpeas

With Vegetables

Chickpea and Beet
Chickpea and Tomato
Chickpea and Pumpkin
Chickpea and Cauliflower
Chickpea and Asparagus
Chickpea and Red Bell Pepper

Chickpea and Sweet Potato
Chickpea and Butternut Squash
Chickpea, Tomato, and Zucchini
Chickpea, Bell Pepper, and Eggplant
Chickpea, Mushroom, and Tomato
Chickpea, Sweet Potato, and Eggplant

Combine purees in equal parts. They taste great warm or cool. Try mixing yummy combo with a little breast milk, formula, or stock and a baby cereal or grain (rice, barley, millet, amaranth, or quinoa). These combos will stay fresh in your cooler, with the frozen ice pack, for 12 hours and out of the refrigerator or cooler for 2 hours.

With Meat

Chickpea, Pumpkin, and Lamb, Pork, Poultry, or Beef
Chickpea, Tomato, Zucchini, and Lamb, Pork, Poultry, or Beef
Chickpea, Butternut Squash, and Lamb, Pork, Poultry, or Beef
Chickpea, Eggplant, Bell Pepper, and Lamb, Pork, Poultry, or Beef

Combine purees in equal parts. They should be served warm. Try mixing yummy combo with a little stock and a baby cereal or grain (rice, millet, barley, amaranth, or quinoa). These combos should not be out of the refrigerator for more than 1 hour.

10-12 MONTHS

spinach

1 lb of Fresh Spinach = 8 oz puree

EXCELLENT SOURCE OF:
VITAMIN K
VITAMIN A
FOLATE

GOOD SOURCE OF:
VITAMIN C
MANGANESE
MAGNESIUM
IRON
POTASSIUM

ALSO CONTAINS:
FIBER
VITAMIN E
RIBOFLAVIN
VITAMIN B6
CALCIUM
PROTEIN
THIAMIN
COPPER
NIACIN
PHOSPHORUS
SODIUM
ZINC

SUITABLE FOR
REFRIGERATOR
AND FREEZER

* Put spinach leaves in strainer and wash thoroughly under cold running water.
* Place spinach in steamer basket and steam for about 5 minutes, until wilted (10 minutes if using frozen).
* Puree until chunk-a-licious using a food processor. Add a little breast milk, formula, purified water or stock, as needed, to thin puree.
* Let cool and serve or store.
* Spinach puree can be stored in Sage Spoonfuls jars for up to 3 days in the refrigerator or up to 3 months in the freezer.

Serving
Spinach puree should be served warm and is best mixed with other food. Try mixing puree with a little breast milk, formula, or stock and a baby cereal or grain (rice, millet, barley, amaranth, or quinoa). Add a pinch of grated cheese for extra flavor.

On-The-Go
Stored in Sage Spoonfuls jars, spinach puree will stay fresh in your cooler, with the frozen ice pack, for up to 12 hours and out of the refrigerator or cooler for up to 2 hours.

All About Spinach
Spinach is packed with vitamins and nutrients. It has more iron than most greens and is rich in lutein, which is good for your baby's eyesight. Additionally, spinach has strong anticancer properties. Conventionally grown spinach is high in nitrates; buy organic whenever possible. Look for fresh spinach with brightly colored green leaves that show no signs of wilting or decay. Spinach will stay fresh in a sealed container in the refrigerator for about 1 week. Frozen spinach is also great to use.

Yummy Combinations With Spinach

With Fruit

Spinach and Pear
Spinach and Apple

Combine purees in equal parts. They taste great warm or cool. Try mixing yummy combo with a little breast milk or formula and a baby cereal or grain (rice, millet, barley, amaranth, or quinoa) and serve warm. These combos will stay fresh in your cooler, with the frozen ice pack, for 12 hours and out of the refrigerator or cooler for 2 hours.

With Vegetables And Beans

Spinach and Potato
Spinach and Carrot
Spinach and Parsnip
Spinach and Sweet Potato
Spinach and Butternut Squash
Spinach, Beet, and Potato

Spinach, Pea, and Pear
Spinach, Lentil, and Pumpkin
Spinach, Chickpea, and Tomato
Spinach, Mushroom, and Potato
Spinach, Sweet Potato, and Pea
Spinach, Split Pea, Tomato, and Carrot

Combine purees in equal parts. They taste best when served warm. Try mixing yummy combo with a little breast milk, formula, or stock and a baby cereal or grain (rice, millet, barley, amaranth, or quinoa). For extra flavor, add a pinch of parsley or grated cheese. These combos will stay fresh in your cooler, with the frozen ice pack, for 12 hours and out of the refrigerator or cooler for 2 hours.

With Meat

Spinach, Zucchini, Tomato, and Fish
Spinach, Mushroom, Carrot, and Beef or Lamb
Spinach, Potato, and Poultry, Pork, Lamb, Beef, or Fish
Spinach, Butternut Squash, and Poultry, Pork, Lamb, or Beef

Combine purees in equal parts. They taste best warm. Try mixing yummy combo with a little stock and a baby cereal or grain (rice, barley, millet, amaranth, or quinoa). For extra flavor, add a pinch of fresh parsley or sage. These combos should not be out of the refrigerator for more than 1 hour.

lima beans

2 Cups Frozen Lima Beans = 8 oz puree

* Place lima beans in steamer basket and steam for 7–10 minutes.
* Puree until chunk-a-licious using a food processor or the back of a fork. Add cooking water or stock, as needed, to thin puree.
* Let cool and serve or store.
* Lima bean puree puree can be stored in Sage Spoonfuls jars for up to 3 days in the refrigerator or up to 3 months in the freezer.

Serving
Lima Bean puree can be served warm or cool and is best mixed with other foods. Try mixing puree with a little breast milk, formula, or stock and a baby cereal or grain (rice, barley, millet, amaranth, or quinoa) and serve warm. It can also be mixed with yogurt or cottage cheese and served cool.

On-The-Go
Stored in Sage Spoonfuls jars, lima bean puree will stay fresh in your cooler, with the frozen ice pack, for up to 12 hours and out of the refrigerator or cooler for up to 2 hours (1 hour when mixed with yogurt or cottage cheese).

All About Lima Beans
Lima beans are a true superfood. They are packed with heart-healthy nutrients, cholesterol lowering fiber, and cancer-fighting antioxidants. Lima beans are also rich in non-meat protein, making them a great choice for babies on a vegetarian diet. Lima bean puree has a potato-like consistency and a buttery taste that blends well with many different foods. Dried lima beans can be purchased in bulk and will stay fresh in an airtight container in a cool, dry place for up to 1 year. I like to use frozen lima beans, because they cook so quickly.

EXCELLENT SOURCE OF:
FOLATE
MANGANESE
FIBER
MAGNESIUM
POTASSIUM
PROTEIN
IRON
PHOSPHORUS
COPPER
THIAMIN
VITAMIN B6
ZINC
PANTOTHENIC ACID
RIBOFLAVIN
CARBOHYDRATES

GOOD SOURCE OF:
SELENIUM
CALCIUM
NIACIN
VITAMIN K

ALSO CONTAINS:
VITAMIN E
SODIUM

SUITABLE FOR
REFRIGERATOR
AND FREEZER

Yummy Combinations With Lima Beans

With Fruit

Lima Bean and Apricot
Lima Bean and Peach

Combine purees in equal parts. They taste best warm, but can also be served cool. Try mixing yummy combo with a little breast milk or formula and a baby cereal or grain (rice, barley, millet, amaranth or quinoa) and serve warm. These combos can also be mixed with yogurt or cottage cheese and served cool. They will stay fresh in your cooler, with the frozen ice pack, for 12 hours and out of the refrigerator or cooler for 2 hours (1 hour when mixed with yogurt or cottage cheese).

With Vegetables

Lima Bean and Potato   Lima Bean and Sweet Potato
Lima Bean and Carrot   Lima Bean and Butternut Squash
Lima Bean and Parsnip   Lima Bean, Corn, and Tomato
Lima Bean and Beet   Lima Bean, Leek, and Potato
Lima Bean and Corn   Lima Bean, Carrot, and Beet

Combine purees in equal parts. They taste great warm or cool. Try mixing yummy combo with a little breast milk, formula, or stock and a baby cereal or grain (rice, barley, millet, amaranth, or quinoa). For extra flavor, add a pinch of grated cheese. These combos will stay fresh in your cooler, with the frozen ice pack, for 12 hours and out of the refrigerator or cooler for 2 hours.

With Meat

Lima Bean, Corn, Tomato, and Fish
Lima Bean, Apricot, Prune, and Lamb or Beef
Lima Bean, Sweet Potato, and Poultry, Pork, Lamb, or Beef
Lima Bean, Beet, Potato and Poultry, Pork, Lamb, Beef, or Fish
Lima Bean, Butternut Squash, and Poultry, Pork, Lamb, or Beef

Combine purees in equal parts. They should be served warm. Try mixing yummy combo with a little stock and a baby cereal or grain (rice, barley, millet, amaranth, or quinoa). For extra flavor, add a pinch of fresh parsley or sage. These combos should not be out of the refrigerator for more than 1 hour.

10-12 MONTHS

bell peppers

1 Bell Pepper = 4 oz puree

* Wash pepper thoroughly under cold running water, cut in half, remove seeds and stem and discard.
* Chop pepper, place in steamer basket and steam for 5–7 minutes, until tender.
* Puree until chunk-a-licious using a food processor. Add purified water or stock, as needed, to thin puree.
* Let cool and serve or store.
* Bell pepper puree puree can be stored in Sage Spoonfuls jars for up to 3 days in the refrigerator or up to 3 months in the freezer.

Serving
Bell pepper puree can be served warm or cool and is best mixed with other food. Try mixing puree with a little breast milk, formula, or stock and a baby cereal or grain (rice, barley, millet, amaranth, or quinoa) and serve warm. It can also be mixed with yogurt, silken tofu, ricotta, or cottage cheese and served cool. Bell peppers can mixed with small shaped pasta. For extra flavor, add a pinch of grated cheese

On-The-Go
Stored in Sage Spoonfuls jars, bell pepper puree will stay fresh in your cooler, with the frozen ice pack, for up to 12 hours and out of the refrigerator or cooler for up to 2 hours (1 hour when mixed with yogurt, tofu, or cheese).

All About Bell Peppers
Bell peppers are rich in nutrients, especially Vitamin C and antioxidants. They come in many different varieties with red being the sweetest and highest in nutrients. Bell Peppers also contain lycopene, which is known to protect against heart disease and cancer. Gently steamed, bite sized pieces of bell pepper make a great finger food for this stage. Look for bell peppers that are rich in color, heavy for their size, and firm to the touch. They will stay fresh in the refrigerator for up to 1 week.

10–12 MONTHS AND UP

EXCELLENT SOURCE OF:
VITAMIN C
VITAMIN A
VITAMIN B6
FOLATE

GOOD SOURCE OF:
FIBER
VITAMIN E
VITAMIN K
POTASSIUM
MANGANESE
RIBOFLAVIN
NIACIN
THIAMIN
PANTOTHENIC ACID

ALSO CONTAINS:
IRON
MAGNESIUM
PHOSPHORUS
PROTEIN
ZINC
CALCIUM
COPPER

SUITABLE FOR REFRIGERATOR AND FREEZER

Yummy Combinations With Bell Peppers

With Vegetables

Bell Pepper and Pea
Bell Pepper and Parsnip
Bell Pepper and Carrot
Bell Pepper and Zucchini
Bell Pepper and Potato

Bell Pepper and Eggplant
Bell Pepper and Cauliflower
Bell Pepper, Mushroom, and Broccoli
Bell Pepper, Eggplant, and Zucchini
Bell Pepper, Corn, and Sweet Potato

Combine purees in equal parts. They can be served warm or cool. Try mixing yummy combo with a little breast milk, formula or stock and a baby cereal or grain (rice, barley, millet, amaranth or quinoa) and serve warm. With the exception of potato and sweet potato, these combos can also be mixed with small shaped pasta. For extra flavor, add a pinch of fresh basil or grated cheese. These combos will stay fresh in your cooler, with the frozen ice pack, for 12 hours and out of the refrigerator or cooler for 2 hours.

With Beans

Bell Pepper and Lentil
Bell Pepper and Black Bean
Bell Pepper, Carrot, and Black Bean
Bell Pepper, Eggplant, and Chickpea
Bell Pepper, Mango, and Black Bean

Combine purees in equal parts. They taste best warm, but can also be served cool. Try mixing yummy combo with a little stock and a baby cereal or grain (rice, barley, millet, amaranth or quinoa) and serve warm. For extra flavor, add a pinch of fresh basil or parsley. These combos will stay fresh in your cooler, with the frozen ice pack, for 12 hours and out of the refrigerator or cooler for 2 hours.

With Meat

Bell Pepper, Zucchini, and Fish
Bell Pepper, Mango, and Chicken or Turkey
Bell Pepper, Lima Bean, Corn, and Fish
Bell Pepper, Cauliflower, and Chicken, Turkey, or Pork
Bell Pepper, Eggplant, and Chicken, Turkey, or Fish
Bell Pepper, Asparagus, and Chicken, Turkey, or Fish

Combine purees in equal parts. They should be served warm. Try mixing yummy combo with a little stock and a baby cereal or grain (rice, barley, millet, amaranth, or quinoa). These combos can also be mixed with small shaped pasta. For extra flavor, add a pinch of fresh parsley. These combos should not be out of the refrigerator for more than 1 hour.

mushrooms

1 Cup Mushrooms = 3 oz puree

10–12 MONTHS AND UP

EXCELLENT SOURCE OF:
RIBOFLAVIN
NIACIN
COPPER
SELENIUM
PANTOTHENIC ACID

GOOD SOURCE OF:
POTASSIUM
PHOSPHOROUS
MANGANESE
FOLATE
FIBER

ALSO CONTAINS:
PROTEIN
THIAMIN
VITAMIN B6
ZINC
IRON
MAGNESIUM
VITAMIN B12
CALCIUM

❄
SUITABLE FOR
REFRIGERATOR
AND FREEZER

* Place mushrooms in strainer and wash thoroughly under cold running water. Pat dry with a paper towel and chop.
* Place mushrooms in steamer basket and steam for 5–7 minutes, (10 minutes if using frozen).
* Puree until chunk-a-licious using a food processor or finely chop with a knife.
* Let cool and serve or store.
* Mushroom puree puree can be stored in Sage Spoonfuls jars for up to 3 days in the refrigerator or up to 3 months in the freezer.

Serving
Mushroom puree should be served warm and is best mixed with other food. Try mixing puree with a little stock and a baby cereal or grain (rice, barley, millet, amaranth or quinoa). It can also be mixed with small shaped pasta. For extra flavor, add a pinch of fresh parsley or grated cheese.

On-The-Go
Stored in Sage Spoonfuls jars, mushroom puree will stay fresh in your cooler, with the frozen ice pack, for up to 12 hours and out of the refrigerator or cooler for up to 2 hours.

All About Mushrooms
Mushrooms come in many varieties—Portobello, white, and crimini are my favorites. Actually, Portobello mushrooms are just overgrown criminis. Portobellos have a more meaty flavor and texture; they are a great food for vegetarian babies because they contain vitamin B12, which is found mostly in poultry and meat. White mushrooms have a mild flavor and criminis have a stronger flavor. Look for mushrooms that are firm and fresh looking. They will stay fresh in their package for about 1 week in the refrigerator. Frozen mushrooms are a good choice as well.

Yummy Combinations With Mushrooms

With Vegetables

Mushroom, Pea, and Carrot
Mushroom, Leek, and Eggplant
Mushroom, Spinach, and Potato
Mushroom, Broccoli, and Sweet Potato
Mushroom, Green Bean, and Potato
Mushroom, Bell Pepper, and Asparagus

Combine purees in equal parts. They taste best warm, but can also be served cool. Try mixing yummy combo with a little stock and a baby cereal or grain (rice, barley, millet, amaranth, or quinoa). For extra flavor, add a pinch of fresh thyme, parsley, or grated cheese. These combos will stay fresh in your cooler, with the frozen ice pack, for 12 hours and out of the refrigerator or cooler for 2 hours.

With Beans

Mushroom, Tomato, and Split Pea or Lentil
Mushroom, Leek, Carrot, and Split Pea or Lentil
Mushroom, Butternut Squash, and Split Pea, Lentil, or Chickpea
Mushroom, Eggplant, Tomato, and Split Pea, Lentil, or Chickpea

Combine purees in equal parts. They should be served warm. Try mixing yummy combo with a little stock and a baby cereal or grain (rice, barley, millet, amaranth, or quinoa). These combos will stay fresh in your cooler, with the frozen ice pack, for 12 hours and out of the refrigerator or cooler for 2 hours.

With Meat

Mushroom, Beet, and Beef or Lamb
Mushroom, Zucchini, Bell Pepper, and Fish
Mushroom, Carrot, and Poultry, Pork, Beef, or Lamb
Mushroom, Parsnip, Pea, and Poultry, Pork, Beef, or Lamb
Mushroom, Leek, Potato, and Poultry, Pork, Beef, or Lamb
Mushroom, Spinach, Potato, and Poultry, Pork, Beef, or Lamb

Combine purees in equal parts. They should be served warm. Try mixing yummy combo with a little stock and a baby cereal or grain (rice, barley, millet, amaranth, or quinoa). For extra flavor, add a pinch of fresh parsley, rosemary, or sage These combos should not be out of the refrigerator for more than 1 hour.

EXCELLENT SOURCE OF:

PROTEIN

VITAMIN B12

POTASSIUM

ZINC

SELENIUM

PANTOTHENIC ACID

MAGNESIUM

GOOD SOURCE OF:

NIACIN

IRON

PHOSPHORUS

VITAMIN B6

RIBOFLAVIN

THIAMIN

COPPER

FOLATE

CALCIUM

SODIUM

VITAMIN E

VITAMIN K

ALSO CONTAINS:

MANGANESE

SUITABLE FOR
REFRIGERATOR
AND FREEZER

beef

1 Lb Ground Beef = 16 oz cooked

* Pour 1 cup of purified water or stock into a medium skillet. Bring to a boil over medium–high heat.

* Add ground beef and cook for about 3 minutes until cooked through and no longer pink. Break the meat up with the end of a spatula during cooking to keep the pieces small.

* Remove beef from skillet using a slotted spoon.

* The ground beef should be chunk-a-licious after cooking; use a food processor or the back of a fork to puree further, if neccessary.

* Let cool and serve or store.

* Beef puree can be stored in Sage Spoonfuls jars for up to 3 days in the refrigerator and up to 1 month in the freezer.

Serving
Beef puree should be served warm and is best mixed with other food. Try mixing puree with a little stock and a baby cereal or grain (rice, barley, millet, amaranth, or quinoa). It can also be mixed with small shaped pasta. For extra flavor, add a pinch of fresh thyme, ginger, turmeric, or grated cheese.

On-The-Go
Beef puree should not be out of the refrigerator for more than 1 hour.

All About Beef
Whenever possible, buy organic, grass fed beef—it is higher in omega 3's and protein then corn-fed and is usually leaner. As pre-packaged ground beef is usually not organic or grass fed, you can ask the butcher to grind a tenderloin or other whole piece for you. Choose lean cuts of red meat for your baby—fatty cuts are high in cholesterol and have been linked to heart disease and cancer. However, lean red meat has about the same amount of cholesterol as poultry. Look for meat that is bright red in color and be sure to check the freshness date. Avoid any meat that looks dull or gray. Put it in the refrigerator or freezer as soon as you get home. When wrapped properly, raw beef will stay fresh for 3 days in the refrigerator and up to 3 months in the freezer.

Yummy Combinations With Beef

With Fruit

Beef and Apricot
Beef and Mango

Combine purees in equal parts. They should be served warm. Try mixing yummy combo with a little breast milk, formula or stock and a baby cereal or grain (rice, millet, amaranth or quinoa). These combos should not be out of the refrigerator for more than 1 hour.

With Vegetables

Beef and Broccoli
Beef and Potato
Beef and Sweet Potato
Beef and Pumpkin
Beef and Green Bean
Beef and Butternut Squash
Beef, Potato, and Pea
Beef, Carrot, and Corn
Beef, Spinach, and Potato

Beef, Broccoli, and Parsnip
Beef, Potato, Leek, and Pea
Beef, Eggplant, and Zucchini
Beef, Mushroom, and Spinach
Beef, Mushroom, and Asparagus
Beef, Mango, and Bell Pepper
Beef, Lima Bean, and Apricot
Beef, Cauliflower, and Broccoli
Beef, Green Bean, and Sweet Potato

Combine purees in equal parts. They should be served warm. Try mixing yummy combo with a little stock and a baby cereal or grain (rice, barley, millet, amaranth, or quinoa). For extra flavor, add a pinch of fresh parsley, thyme, garlic, turmeric, or grated cheese. These combos should not be out of the refrigerator or more than 1 hour.

salmon

½ Lb Salmon (skin removed) = 8 oz puree

EXCELLENT SOURCE OF:
VITAMIN B12
NIACIN
PROTEIN
SELENIUM
PHOSPHORUS
VITAMIN B6
VITAMIN E
PANTOTHENIC ACID
THIAMIN
POTASSIUM
RIBOFLAVIN

GOOD SOURCE OF:
VITAMIN C
MAGNESIUM
FOLATE
SODIUM
ZINC

ALSO CONTAINS:
IRON
COPPER
VITAMIN A
VITAMIN K
CALCIUM
MANGANESE

SUITABLE FOR
REFRIGERATOR
AND FREEZER

* Bring 1 cup of purified water or stock to a boil in a medium skillet over medium–high heat
* Place salmon in skillet and cook for about 3 minutes on each side until opaque all the way through.
* Remove the salmon from the skillet, using a spatula or slotted spoon and place in a bowl
* Mash until chunk-a-licious with the back of a fork.
* Let cool and serve or store.
* Salmon puree can be stored in Sage Spoonfuls jars for up to 2 days in the refrigerator and up to 1 month in the freezer.
* To roast: Place salmon on a baking sheet lined with parchment paper, roast at 375 for about 20–25 minutes, until opaque all the way through; mash until chunk-a-licious with the back of a fork.

Serving
Salmon puree should be served warm and is best mixed with other food. Try mixing puree with a little vegetable stock and a baby cereal or grain (rice, barley, millet, amaranth, or quinoa). For extra flavor, add a pinch of fresh parsley or basil.

On-The-Go
Salmon puree should not be out of the refrigerator for more than 1 hour.

All About Salmon
Salmon is a wonderful fish for your baby—it is low in mercury and is rich in nutrients, including Vitamin B12. Additionally, it is one of the best natural sources of DHA; just 2 servings per week will meet your baby's Omega 3 needs. Whenever possible, buy wild Alaskan salmon. Look for salmon that is firm with a rich orange color and avoid any that smells "fishy". Salmon will stay fresh in the refrigerator for up to 2 days, when wrapped properly.

Yummy Combinations With Salmon

With Vegetables

Salmon and Potato
Salmon and Asparagus
Salmon and Zucchini
Salmon and Butternut Squash
Salmon, Pea, and Carrot

Salmon, Zucchini, and Tomato
Salmon, Spinach, and Potato
Salmon, Mango, and Tomato
Salmon, Asparagus, and Potato
Salmon, Corn, and Bell Pepper

Combine purees in equal parts. They should be served warm. Try mixing yummy combo with a little stock and a baby cereal (rice, barley, millet, amaranth, or quinoa). For extra flavor, add a pinch of fresh parsley or basil. These combos should not be out of the refrigerator for more than 1 hour.

With Beans

Salmon and Lentil or Split Pea
Salmon, Corn, and Lima Bean
Salmon, Butternut Squash, and Lentil
Salmon, Carrot, and Lentil or Split Pea
Salmon, Tomato, Leek, and Lentil or Split Pea
Salmon, Tomato, Zucchini, and Lentil or Split Pea

Combine purees in equal parts. They should be served warm. Try mixing yummy combo with a little stock and a baby cereal or grain (rice, barley, millet, amaranth, or quinoa). For extra flavor, add a pinch of fresh parsley or basil. These combos should not be out of the refrigerator for more than 1 hour.

Notes:

FAMILY FAVORITES

FAMILY
FAVORITES

Family Favorites

This chapter includes some of my family's favorite recipes. The beauty of these recipes is that they are ones the entire family, babies and toddlers included, can enjoy together.

There is nothing I find more comforting and enjoyable than sitting down to a meal with my family. I hope you enjoy sharing these recipes with your family as much as I enjoy sharing them with mine.

✱ When serving family favorites to your baby or toddler, keep in mind the textures that are appropriate for each stage:

* ✱ 4–6 Months – Smooth and Creamy
* ✱ 7–9 Months – Mushy mash
* ✱ 10–12 Months – Chunk-a-licious
* ✱ Toddlers – finely chopped or bite sized

infused water

Serves 6 to 8

Cucumber Mint

* Wash cucumber thoroughly under cold running water.
* Slice into thin rounds and place into a pitcher along with the mint. Fill pitcher with water.
* Place pitcher in refrigerator and chill for a few hours or overnight.
* Stir before serving.

Mango Peach

* Wash mango and peach thoroughly under cold running water.
* Slice mango and peach into wedges and place in pitcher. Fill pitcher with water.
* Place pitcher in refrigerator and chill for a few hours or overnight.
* Stir before serving.

Pear

* Wash pears thoroughly under cold running water.
* Slice pear away from the core. Discard core and cut pears into wedges.
* Put pear into a pitcher and fill with water.
* Place pitcher in refrigerator and chill for a few hours or overnight.
* Stir before serving.

Serving
Infused waters are best served cold. For a baby 4–12 months, place in a bottle, for a toddler place in a sippy cup, and for an adult, place in a glass with ice and pieces of the fruit or cucumber and mint.

On-The-Go
Infused water stays fresh all day.

All About Infused water
These delicious infused waters are a wonderful way to stay hydrated on a hot day. They are also perfect for when your baby or toddler isn't feeling well and needs extra hydration. These waters have a yummy hint of flavor, but without the high sugar and calorie content of juice. Your baby, and the rest of your family, will love the refreshing taste. Whenever possible, use organic cucumbers and fruit when making infused water, because you will be leaving the skin on.

4–6 MONTHS AND UP

INGREDIENT LIST:

CUCUMBER MINT

1 MEDIUM CUCUMBER
3 SPRIGS FRESH MINT
8–10 CUPS
  PURIFIED WATER

MANGO-PEACH

1 MANGO
1 PEACH
8–10 CUPS
  PURIFIED WATER

PEAR

2 BARTLETT PEARS
8–10 CUPS
  PURIFIED WATER

❄

SUITABLE FOR
REFRIGERATOR

7–9 MONTHS AND UP

INGREDIENT LIST:

1 CUP OF ORGANIC, WHOLE MILK VANILLA YOGURT

1 MEDIUM RIPE BANANA

½ CUP OF FROZEN ORGANIC BLUEBERRIES

HANDFUL OF ICE CUBES

*7–9 MONTHS: YOU CAN SUBSTITUTE MANGO, PEACH, PLUM, APRICOT, CHERRY, OR PRUNE FOR THE BLUEBERRIES.

*10–12 MONTHS: YOU CAN SUBSTITUTE STRAWBERRIES, PINEAPPLE, KIWI, BLACK-BERRIES, OR RASPBERRIES FOR THE BLUEBERRIES. YOU CAN ALSO SUBSTITUTE SILKEN TOFU FOR THE VANILLA YOGURT.

*OVER 12 MONTHS: WHOLE MILK CAN BE SUBSTITUTED FOR THE TOFU OR YOGURT.

❄

SUITABLE FOR REFRIGERATOR AND FREEZER

it's smoothie time!

Serves 2–3

✳ Blend ingredients together until smooth in a standard blender.

✳ Serve or store

✳ While smoothies are best when served immediately after preparing, they can be stored in Sage Spoonfuls jars for up to 3 days in the refrigerator or 3 months in the freezer.

Serving
Smoothies are best served cold. For a baby 7–12 months, serve with a spoon as you would a puree or put it in a bottle with a Y-cut nipple. For a toddler, you can put the smoothie in a sippy cup that has a Y-cut or straw top. For an adult, serve in a tall glass.

On-The-Go
Stored in Sage Spoonfuls jars, smoothies will stay fresh and chilled in your cooler, with the frozen ice pack, for up to 12 hours and out of the refrigerator or cooler for 1 hour.

All About Smoothies
Smoothies are a big hit in my family. Every time I yell out, "it's smoothie time!" the kids come running. Smoothies are a delicious way to fill your family's bellies with nutrients. Even when my kids aren't feeling well and don't have much of an appetite, they still always drink their smoothies. It's a great way to keep them hydrated while giving them added nutrients. For infants, smoothies are a wonderful treat on a warm day or as a healthy way to soothe sore gums. For children and adults, smoothies make a quick and satisfying breakfast or snack.

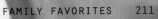

chicken soup pasta

Serves 2 Adults and 2 Children

INGREDIENT LIST:

2 CARROTS, WASHED, PEELED, DICED

2 CELERY STALKS, WASHED, DICED

2 BONELESS SKINLESS CHICKEN BREASTS, DICED

1 CUP OF PASTINA OR OTHER SMALL SHAPED PASTA

4 CUPS OF LOW SODIUM CHICKEN OR VEGETABLE STOCK

PINCH OF KOSHER OR COARSE SEA SALT (OPTIONAL)

SUITABLE FOR REFRIGERATOR AND FREEZER

* Pour 2 cups of the stock into a medium saucepan and bring to a boil over high heat.

* Add the chicken and cook for 2–3 minutes, until no longer pink inside.

* Remove chicken from the saucepan with a slotted spoon and set aside in a bowl; discard stock.

* Pour remaining 2 cups of stock into the saucepan and bring to a boil over high heat. Add pastina and let boil for 7–10 minutes, stirring occasionally.

* While the pasta is cooking, steam the carrots and celery for about 7 minutes. Remove from steamer basket and set aside in a bowl.

* Once the pasta is cooked, add the chicken, carrots, and celery to the saucepan and stir to combine. If desired, add extra stock for a more soup-like consistency, or a pinch of salt.

* Serve or store.

* Chicken soup pasta can be stored in Sage Spoonfuls jars for up to 3 days in the refrigerator and up to 3 months in the freezer.

Serving
Chicken soup pasta should be served warm. For extra flavor, add a pinch of fresh parsley or grated parmesan cheese. For a baby 7–12 months, puree the carrot, celery, and chicken to a consistency your baby can handle before adding to the pastina. For a toddler, be sure the pieces of chicken are bite sized before mixing with pastina. For an adult, serve in a bowl.

On-The-Go
Chicken soup pasta should not be out of the refrigerator for more than 1 hour.

All About Chicken Soup Pasta
Chicken soup is one of the most comforting and wholesome meals you can make when someone you love isn't feeling well. However, soup is a little difficult to feed a baby. When Royce was an infant and he got his first cold, I had the idea to make this chicken "soup" pasta. It has all the nutrients and comfort of soup, but with a thicker consistency that a baby can handle. It remains a favorite in our house, whenever someone isn't feeling well, or as a yummy, warm meal on a cold day.

apricot lamb curry

Serves 2 Adults and 2 Children

* Preheat oven to 400 and line a baking sheet with unbleached parchment paper.
* Bring 2 cups of vegetable stock to a boil in a medium saucepan over high heat. Add the brown rice or quinoa and let boil for 1 minute. Reduce heat to low, cover, and simmer for 30 minutes, until all the liquid is absorbed. Add more stock if needed.
* Place lamb chops onto baking sheet, brush lightly with olive oil, and season with salt and pepper. Place baking sheet in the oven on the center rack. Roast lamb chops for 20 minutes; remove from oven and let sit for 5 minutes.
* While the rice/quinoa and lamb are cooking, bring the coconut milk to a near-boil in a small saucepan, over medium–high heat. Add the apricots and curry powder, reduce heat to low, and simmer for about 10 minutes, stirring frequently. Add a pinch of salt and pepper, if desired.
* While the apricot curry is cooking, steam asparagus for about 7 minutes, until bright green and tender.
* Serve or store.
* While this meal is best served immediately after preparing, it will stay fresh in an air tight container in the refrigerator for up to 3 days in the refrigerator and up to 1 month in the freezer.

Serving
Apricot lamb curry should be served warm. For a baby 7–12 months, cut the lamb off the bone and place into a food processor with the rice/quinoa, asparagus, and a little apricot curry sauce. Pulse until the appropriate consistency is achieved. For a toddler, serve bite size pieces of lamb with curry sauce and asparagus alongside the rice or quinoa. For an adult, spoon apricot curry over the lamb chops and serve alongside rice/quinoa and the asparagus.

On-The-Go
Apricot lamb curry should not be out of the refrigerator for more than 1 hour.

All About Apricot Lamb Curry
This dish is an easy and delicious way to introduce curry to your family. The apricots pair incredibly well with the coconut milk and lamb, giving the curry an unexpected taste of sweetness!

7–9 MONTHS AND UP

FAMILY FAVORITES

INGREDIENT LIST:

1 BUNCH OF FRESH ASPARAGUS

1 CUP BROWN RICE OR QUINOA

2 CUPS LOW-SODIUM VEGETABLE STOCK

1 TEASPOON YELLOW CURRY POWDER

1½ CUPS COCONUT MILK

6–8 RIB LAMB CHOPS, 1" THICK

½ CUP DRIED APRICOTS, DICED

1 TEASPOON OLIVE OIL

PINCH OF KOSHER OR SEA SALT AND PEPPER (OPTIONAL)

❄

SUITABLE FOR REFRIGERATOR AND FREEZER

INGREDIENT LIST:

2 TABLESPOONS EXTRA VIRGIN OLIVE OIL

1 SMALL YELLOW ONION, FINELY CHOPPED

2–4 CLOVES OF MINCED GARLIC

2 28 OUNCE CANS OF CRUSHED TOMATOES (BPA FREE CANS, WHENEVER POSSIBLE)

1 BAY LEAF

1 TABLESPOON OF DRIED OREGANO (2 TABLSPOONS IF USING FRESH)

1 TABLESPOON OF DRIED BASIL (2 TABLESPOONS IF USING FRESH)

1 VEGETABLE BOUILLON CUBE

❄

SUITABLE FOR REFRIGERATOR AND FREEZER

too good to be true tomato sauce

Serves 8–10

* Heat the olive oil in a large pot over medium–high heat.

* Add the onion and garlic, reduce heat to medium, and cook for 10 minutes, stirring frequently. The onions and garlic should not brown—you just want them to become translucent.

* Add bouillon cube and combine into onion and garlic, 1 minute.

* Add crushed tomatoes, bay leaf, oregano, and basil. Raise heat to high and bring to a boil.

* Let boil for one minute, then reduce heat to low, partially cover and let simmer for 45 minutes, stirring occasionally. During this time, the sauce will cook down and the flavors will combine.

* Serve or store.

* This tomato sauce can be stored in an airtight container for up to 3 days in the refrigerator and up to 3 months in the freezer.

Serving
This tomato sauce is delicious on all types of pasta. At 7–9 months, stick with small shapes like pastina and stellini. At 10–12 months, you can move to slightly bigger shapes like orzo, ditallini, and alphabet pasta, if your baby is ready. For extra flavor, add some grated parmesan cheese and a pinch of fresh basil or parsley.

On-The-Go
Stored in Sage Spoonfuls jars, tomato sauce will stay fresh in your cooler, with the frozen ice pack, for up to 12 hours and out of the refrigerator or cooler for 2 hours.

All About Tomato Sauce
This tomato sauce is full of nutrients and packed with flavor. Tomatoes and oregano, in particular, are rich sources of disease-fighting antioxidants. For added nutrition, try different grain pastas like kamut, quinoa, and, for babies over 12 months, whole wheat; these pastas have a much higher nutrient content than white pasta. Tomato sauce and pasta is a great "go-to" dish. This recipe yields a large amount of sauce—you can store what is leftover and keep it in the freezer for future meals. This recipe has been in my family for generations. It is simple to make and has a fantastic flavor. I hope you enjoy it as much as we do!

FAMILY
FAVORITES

INGREDIENT LIST:

3 TABLESPOONS EXTRA VIRGIN OLIVE OIL

2 CARROTS, WASHED, PEELED, AND SLICED

2 POTATOES, WASHED, AND CUBED

1 YELLOW ONION, CUT INTO WEDGES

1 4 LB WHOLE ORGANIC CHICKEN

2 CLOVES OF GARLIC, MINCED

1 LEMON, CUT INTO QUARTERS

3 SPRIGS OF FRESH ROSEMARY

KOSHER OR COARSE SEA SALT, FRESH CRACKED BLACK PEPPER

❄️

SUITABLE FOR REFRIGERATOR AND FREEZER

roast chicken

Serves 2 Adults and 2 Children

* Preheat oven to 425.

* Place onion, carrots, and potatoes into a large roasting pan and toss with 2 tablespoons of the olive oil. Push veggies to the side and place the minced garlic in the middle of the pan.

* Unwrap the chicken. If present, remove and discard the insides (you can always ask the butcher to do this for you). Rinse the chicken under cold running water and pat dry with a towel.

* Place chicken on a cutting board, place the lemon and rosemary inside, tie the legs together with butcher's twine; then brush the outside of the chicken with the remaining olive oil. Season the chicken with salt and pepper.

* Place the chicken in the center of the roasting pan with the veggies around the sides. Place the roasting pan in the oven on the center rack; roast for 45 minutes; then baste the chicken with pan juices and return to the oven for another 25–30 minutes.

* Using oven mitts, remove the chicken from the oven, place on a separate dish, and let stand for 10 minutes; remove veggies from the pan and set aside; squeeze the lemon into the pan and mix well.

* Serve or store.

* Roast chicken can be stored in an airtight container for up to 3 days in the refrigerator and up to 3 months in the freezer.

Serving
This dish is best served warm; however, leftover roast chicken makes a delicious sandwich. For a baby 7–12 months, place some chopped chicken and pan juices in a food processor with the roasted veggies and puree to a consistency he can handle. For toddlers, cut the chicken and veggies into bite size pieces and serve with pan juices. For an adult, spoon pan juices over the chicken and serve alongside the roasted vegetables.

On-The-Go
This meal should not be out of the refrigerator for more than 1 hour.

All About Roast Chicken
A roast chicken with veggies is comfort food at its best. This meal will fill your home with the most delicious aroma you could imagine. The thought of roasting a whole chicken can be intimidating, but you'll be surprised at how easy it is. The oven does most of the work, but you will get all of the praise!

INGREDIENT LIST:

2 TABLESPOONS EXTRA
  VIRGIN OLIVE OIL

2 CARROTS, WASHED,
  PEELED, DICED

1 TOMATO, WASHED,
  PEELED, DICED

2 CELERY STALKS,
  WASHED, DICED

1 SMALL YELLOW
  ONION, DICED

1 YUKON GOLD POTATO,
  DICED

1 TABLESPOON FRESH,
  MINCED SAGE

1 BAY LEAF

1 CUP OF LENTILS

4 CUPS LOW-SODIUM
  VEGETABLE STOCK

2 TEASPOONS KOSHER
  OR COARSE SEA
  SALT (OPTIONAL)

SUITABLE FOR
REFRIGERATOR
AND FREEZER

lentil stew

Serves 2 Adults and 2 Children

✳ Pour olive oil into a large pot and heat over medium–high. Add carrots, celery, onion, sage and 1 teaspoon of the salt. Let the veggies "sweat" for 5–7 minutes while stirring frequently. You don't want them to brown, just to soften.

✳ Add stock, potato, tomato, lentils, and bay leaf. Bring to a boil over high heat and stir. Let boil for 1 minute, then reduce heat to low, partially cover, and simmer for about 45 minutes, stirring occaisionally, until lentils are very tender.

✳ Add stock, as needed, to thin the stew or to achieve a more soup-like consistency. If desired, add remaining teaspoon of salt. Remove bay leaf before serving.

✳ Let cool slightly and serve or store.

✳ Lentil stew can be stored in Sage Spoonfuls jars for up to 3 days in the refrigerator and up to 3 months in the freezer. It will thicken during storage; add stock, as needed, to thin when reheating.

Serving
Lentil stew should be served warm. For a baby 7–12 months, puree the stew with an immersion blender or food processor to a consistency your baby can handle. For a toddler, serve the stew as you would an adult, in a bowl with a pinch of fresh parsley.

On-The-Go
Stored in Sage Spoonfuls jars, lentil stew will stay fresh in your cooler, with the frozen ice pack, for up to 12 hours and out of the refrigerator or cooler for up to 2 hours.

All About Lentil Stew
Lentil stew is packed with vitamins, nutrients, and antioxidants. It is the perfect meal for a chilly day. I especially love this stew after playing in the snow with my boys. You can use red, yellow, or green lentils. Lentil stew is also a great dish for vegetarian babies, because it is an excellent source of non-meat protein. This is a hearty and delicious dish that your whole family will enjoy.

mango pork tenderloin

Serves 2 Adults and 2 Children

✻ Preheat oven to 450 and line a baking sheet with unbleached parchment paper.

✻ Brush the pork tenderloin lightly with olive oil and season with salt and pepper.

✻ Heat olive oil in a large skillet over high heat. Add pork and cook 2–3 minutes on each side. Transfer pork to a baking sheet and place in the oven, on the center rack, and roast for 10–12 minutes. Remove from the oven, transfer pork to a plate, and let sit for 10 minutes.

✻ Combine a small portion of the mangoes and tomatoes in a bowl for the kids and set aside.

✻ Combine the remaining mangoes and tomatoes in a bowl, with the jalapeno and red onion. Squeeze the lime juice into the bowl; sprinkle with a pinch of salt, and mix well.

✻ Serve or store.

✻ This meal is best served immediately after preparing, but will stay fresh in an airtight container in the refrigerator for up to 3 days and in the freezer for up to 3 months.

Serving

This meal should be served warm. For a baby 7–12 months, chop pork and puree in a food processor, with the unseasoned mango and tomatoes; add brown rice or quinoa if desired. For a toddler, be sure the pork, mango, and tomatoes are bite-sized before serving, and serve alongside brown rice or quinoa, and a steamed veggie. For an adult, slice the pork tenderloin into medallions, top with the mango salsa, and serve with brown rice or quinoa and your favorite steamed vegetable.

On-The-Go

This meal should not be out of the refrigerator for more than 1 hour.

All About Mango Pork Tenderloin

This is one of my husband's favorite meals. Roasted pork tenderloin has such a wonderful flavor, as well as being full of protein. The mangoes and tomatoes add a light taste and texture. This is a meal your family will enjoy all year long.

7–9 MONTHS AND UP

INGREDIENT LIST:

2 TABLESPOONS EXTRA VIRGIN OLIVE OIL

1 LB PORK TENDERLOIN WITH SILVER MEMBRANE TRIMMED OFF

1 MANGO, PEELED AND DICED

2 TOMATOES, CHOPPED

1 SMALL JALAPENO PEPPER, DE-SEEDED AND MINCED

¼ RED ONION, FINELY CHOPPED

½ TEASPOON KOSHER OR COARSE SEA SALT

3 TABLESPOONS FRESH LIME JUICE (ABOUT 1 LIME)

KOSHER OR COARSE SEA SALT AND CRACKED BLACK PEPPER FOR SEASONING

SUITABLE FOR REFRIGERATOR AND FREEZER

salmon with garlic & veggies

Serves 2 adults and 2 children

* Heat the olive oil in a large skillet over high heat. Add the onion and garlic.
* Reduce heat to medium and let cook for 10 minutes, stirring frequently. You only want the onions and garlic to sweat, not brown.
* Add the stock and bring to a boil over medium–high.
* Add the tomatoes, zucchini, and basil to the skillet and cook for 2 minutes.
* Add the salmon filets and cook for about 3 minutes on each side, until fish is opaque throughout.
* Serve or store
* While this meal is best served immediately after preparing, it will stay fresh in an airtight container for up to 3 days in the refrigerator or up to 1 month in the freezer.

Serving
This meal should be served warm. For a baby 10–12 months, place the meal in a food processor and pulse until the consistency your baby can handle is achieved; serve with brown rice or quinoa. For toddlers, mash salmon with a fork and make sure the veggies are in bite sized pieces; serve alongside brown rice or quinoa. For an adult, spoon tomato and zucchini mixture over salmon filet and serve alongside brown rice or quinoa.

On-The-Go
This meal should not be out of the refrigerator for more than 1 hour.

All About Salmon and Veggies
This simple and delicious meal is perfect for when the weather starts to get warm and tomatoes are back in season. Salmon is low in mercury, is nutrient rich and has a pleasing taste. This light and tasty dish is full of flavor, even the pickiest toddlers, who normally turn their noses up at fish, will want to give this dish a try!

10–12 MONTHS AND UP

FAMILY FAVORITES

INGREDIENT LIST:

4 SALMON FILETS, 6–8 OZ EACH, SKIN REMOVED

2 TABLESPOONS EXTRA VIRGIN OLIVE OIL

1 SMALL YELLOW ONION, FINELY CHOPPED

2 CLOVES GARLIC, MINCED

4 TOMATOES, PEELED, DE-SEEDED, AND CHOPPED

3 ZUCCHINI, SLICED IN HALF AND CUT INTO SMALL CHUNKS

2 CUPS OF LOW SODIUM VEGETABLE STOCK

2 TABLESPOONS CHOPPED FRESH BASIL

❄

SUITABLE FOR REFRIGERATOR AND FREEZER

hummus

Serves 4

* Place ingredients in food processor and pulse until smooth and creamy. Scrape the sides of the bowl with spoon or spatula and add extra water during pureeing, as needed.

* Serve or store.

* Hummus can be stored in Sage Spoonfuls jars for up to 5 days in the refrigerator.

Serving
Hummus should be served cool as a finger food, with steamed veggies like red bell pepper, green beans, carrots and eggplant. It is also delicious spread on lightly toasted strips of bread like spelt, kamut, or fortified white bread. Try adding a little red pepper or roasted eggplant in the food processor with the hummus. Blend in 1–2 cloves of garlic for a spicier, more traditionally Mediterranean flavor.

On-The-Go
Stored in Sage Spoonfuls jars, hummus will stay fresh in your cooler, with the frozen ice pack, for up to 12 hours and out of the refrigerator or cooler for up to 2 hours.

All About Hunmus
Hummus is a wonderfully nutritious dish from the Mediterranean. It is easy to make, packed with nutrients, and has a smooth, nutty flavor that babies love. Hummus is a great food for vegetarian babies and is also a protein packed snack when on-the-go. It makes a perfect finger food for babies and a delicious dip and sandwich spread for the rest of the family.

10–12 MONTHS AND UP

INGREDIENT LIST:

1½ CUPS CANNED CHICKPEAS, DRAINED AND RINSED (BPA FREE CANS WHENEVER POSSIBLE)

1 TEASPOON OF KOSHER OR SEA SALT

¼ CUP TAHINI (SESAME PASTE) OR EXTRA VIRGIN OLIVE OIL

3 TABLESPOONS FRESHLY SQUEEZED LEMON JUICE (ABOUT 1 LEMON)

2 TABLESPOONS PURIFIED WATER

1–2 CLOVES OF GARLIC (OPTIONAL)

❄
SUITABLE FOR REFRIGERATOR

muscle man stir-fry

Serves 2 adults and 2 children

INGREDIENT LIST:

1 CUP QUINOA

2 CUPS VEGETABLE STOCK OR PURIFIED WATER

2 TABLESPOONS EXTRA VIRGIN OLIVE OIL

1 SMALL YELLOW ONION, FINELY CHOPPED

1 TABLESPOON FRESH GINGER, MINCED

1 TABLESPOON SCALLION, MINCED

1 RED BELL PEPPER, WASHED AND CHOPPED

2 CUPS PORTOBELLO OR CRIMINI MUSHROOMS, WASHED AND SLICED

2 CUPS BROCCOLI FLORETS, WASHED

⅓ CUP PURIFIED WATER

⅓ CUP LOW SODIUM SOY SAUCE

⅓ CUP HOISIN SAUCE

❄

SUITABLE FOR REFRIGERATOR AND FREEZER

✳ Bring the water or stock to a boil in a small saucepan. Add the quinoa and let boil for 1 minute. Reduce heat to low, cover and let simmer for 20 minutes, stirring occasionally, until the liquid is absorbed. Add more water or stock, if needed.

✳ Heat the olive oil in a large skillet over high heat.

✳ Add the onion, ginger, and minced scallion; reduce heat to medium, and let cook for 10 minutes, stirring frequently. You only want them to sweat, not brown.

✳ Add the bell pepper, mushrooms, and broccoli to the skillet. Raise the heat to medium–high and cook, stirring frequently, for 5 minutes.

✳ Remove a portion of veggies and quinoa that you will serve to your baby and set aside.

✳ Add water, soy sauce and hoisin to the pan and cook, stirring frequently, for 2–3 minutes.

✳ Serve or store.

✳ Muscle Man stir fry can be stored in an airtight container for up to 3 days in the refrigerator or up to 3 months in the freezer.

Serving
This meal should be served warm. For variation, add different vegetables, like snap peas and eggplant. For babies 10–12 months, puree the veggies without the sauce then mix with quinoa. For toddlers, be sure the veggies are bite size before serving. For an adult, serve the stir fry and quinoa in a bowl and garnish with sliced scallion.

On-The-Go
This meal will stay fresh in a Sage Spoonfuls jar in the cooler, with the frozen ice pack, for up to 12 hours and out of the refrigerator or cooler for 2 hours.

All About Muscle Man Stir Fry
Sometimes I like to make up fun names for the meals I cook for my kids. My boys are 2 and 4 and are really into super heroes at the moment. It makes them happy to eat something with a fun name and it makes me ecstatic to see them devour a bowl full of veggies and quinoa. When my daughter gets old enough to have this meal, I will probably call it Princess Power Stir Fry.

Notes:

Sources and References

Medical Advisor – Dr. Laura Pagnotta

Dr. Laura Ann Pagnotta is a Board Certified pediatrician and member of the American Academy of Pediatrics. She served as Chief Resident of Pediatrics at Winthrop University Hospital in New York, and was mentored by renowned neonatologist Dr. Renu Aggarwal. Dr. Pagnotta is the proud mother of 3 wonderful boys—Logan, 6, Kai, 4, and Mason, 6 months. She especially enjoys using her personal experiences as a mom to help guide new mothers during the first few years of their children's lives.

For more information, please visit:

Pediatric Health and Information

American Academy of Pediatrics – www.aap.org
World Health Organization – www.who.int

Food Safety and Nutrition

Center for Food Safety and Applied Nutrition – www.Healthfinder.gov
United States Department of Agriculture – www.USDA.gov
Vegetarian Resource Group – www.vrg.org
The American Red Cross – www.Americanredcross.org
Environmental Defense Fund – www.edf.org/seafoodhealth

Pesticide Use and the Benefits of Going Organic

Environmental Working Group – www.ewg.org
Organic Consumers Association – www.Organicconsumers.org
The Pesticide Action Network – www.panna.org

www.Nutritiondata.com   www.USDA.gov
www.Localharvest.org   www.Foodnews.org
www.Whatsonmyfood.org

Allergies and Food Intolerances

American Academy of Pediatrics – www.aap.org
American Academy of Asthma and Immunology – www.aaaai.org
The Food Allergy and Anaphylaxis Network – www.Foodallergy.org
Gluten Intolerance and Celiac Disease – www.Celiac.com.org

Sage Spoonfuls

Simple Recipes ✳ Healthy Meals ✳ Happy Babies

Conceived and written by Liza Huber
Produced by Sage Bears, LLC
Garden City, New York 11530
Info@sagebears.com   Fax 516 977 3120
Copyright © 2011 by Sage Bears, LLC

Printed in China through Colorcraft Ltd., Hong Kong
First printed in 2011

Photography Basia Ambroziak – www.photobybasia.com
Photography Assistant Malgosia Ambroziak
Food and Prop Stylists Warren Friesner & Erick Kuo
Graphic Design Clearlight Interactive Corp – www.clearlightcorp.com
Creative Director Warren Friesner
Senior Designer Erick Kuo
Designer Nok Acharee

Acknowledgments

I want to thank my wonderful "mommy" friends who not only enthusiastically
supported my ideas, but who allowed me to include their gorgeous babies in
my book—Amy McAlea, Robin McDonough, Sarah Phelan, Suzanne Dillmeier,
and Kara Torre.

I especially want to thank my parents and my incredible husband, Alex, for
believing in me and supporting my vision from the very moment I told them
about my idea for Sage Spoonfuls. I am truly grateful.

Most importantly, I want to thank my beautiful children, Royce, Brendan, and
Hayden. I find no greater joy than in being their mom.

Index